BIOZONE

AQA BIOLOGY 1
A-Level Year 1/AS

MODEL ANSWERS

This model answer booklet is a companion publication to provide answers for the activities in the AQA Biology 1 Student Workbook. These answers have been produced as a separate publication to keep the cost of the workbook itself to a minimum. All answers to set questions are provided, but chapter reviews are the student's own and no model answer is set. Working and explanatory notes have been provided where clarification of the answer is appropriate.

ISBN 978-1-927309-21-6

Copyright © 2015 Richard Allan
Seventh printing
Published by **BIOZONE International Ltd**

Additional copies of this Model Answers book may be purchased directly from the publisher.

BIOZONE Learning Media (UK) Ltd.

Telephone local: 01283 530 366
Telephone international: +44 1283 530 366
Fax local: 01283 831 900
Fax international: +44 1283 831 900
Email: sales@biozone.co.uk

www.**BIOZONE**.co.uk

PHOTOCOPYING PROHIBITED

including photocopying under a photocopy licence scheme such as CLA

All rights reserved. No part of this publication may be reproduced, stored in a retrieval system, or transmitted in any form or by any means, electrical, mechanical, **photocopying**, recording or otherwise, without the permission of BIOZONE International Ltd. This workbook may not be re-sold. The conditions of sale specifically prohibit the photocopying of exercises, worksheets, and diagrams from this workbook for any reason.

CONTENTS AQA BIOLOGY 1

Mathematical and Practical Skills in Biology

1. How Do We Do Science? 4
2. Hypotheses and Predictions 4
3. Types of Data 4
4. Making A Qualitative Investigation 4
5. Making A Quantitative Investigation 4
6. Accuracy and Precision 4
7. Working with Numbers 4
8. Fractions, Percentages, and Ratios 4
9. Logs and Exponents 5
10. Properties of Geometric Shapes 5
11. Practising With Data 5
12. Apparatus and Measurement 5
13. Recording Results 5
14. Constructing Tables and Graphs 5
15. What Graph to Use? 6
16. Drawing Bar Graphs 6
17. Drawing Histograms 6
18. Drawing Line Graphs 6
19. Correlation or Causation 6
20. Drawing Scatter Plots 6
21. Interpreting Line Graphs 7
23. Spearman Rank Correlation 7
24. Mean, Median, Mode 7
25. Spread of Data 7
26. Interpreting Sample Variability 7
27. Biological Drawings 8
28. Practising Biological Drawings 8
29. Test Your Understanding 8

Biological molecules

30. Organic Molecules 9
31. The Biochemical Nature of Cells 9
32. The Common Ancestry of Life 9
33. Sugars 9
34. Condensation and Hydrolysis of Sugars 9
35. Colorimetry 9
36. Polysaccharides 9
37. Starch and Cellulose 10
38. Lipids 10
39. Phospholipids 10
40. Amino Acids 10
41. Chromatography 10
42. Protein Shape is Related to Function 10
43. Protein Structure 10
44. Comparing Globular and Fibrous Proteins 10
45. Biochemical Tests 11
46. Enzymes 11
47. How Enzymes Work 11
48. Models of Enzyme Activity 11
49. Enzyme Kinetics 11
50. Investigating Enzyme Reaction Rates 11
51. Enzyme Inhibitors 11
52. Investigating Catalase Activity 12
53. Nucleotides 12
54. Nucleic Acids 12
55. Determining the Structure of DNA 12
56. Constructing a DNA Model 13
57. DNA Replication 13
58. Enzyme Control of DNA Replication 13
59. Meselson and Stahl's Experiment 13
60. Modelling DNA Replication 14
61. ATP - A Nucleotide Derivative 14
62. Water 14
63. The Properties of Water 14
64. Inorganic Ions 14
65. Chapter Review 14
66. KEY TERMS: Did You Get It? 14

Cells

67. The Cell is the Unit of Life 15
68. Cell Sizes 15
69. Bacterial Cells 15
70. Plant Cells 15
71. Identifying Structures in a Plant Cell 15
72. Animal Cells 15
73. Identifying Structures in an Animal Cell 15
74. Cell Structures and Organelles 15
75. Cell Fractionation 16
76. Identifying Organelles 16
77. Specialisation in Plant Cells 16
78. Specialisation in Human Cells 16
79. Levels of Organisation 17
80. Animal Tissues 17
81. Plant Tissues 17
82. Viruses 17
83. Optical Microscopes 17
84. Preparing a Slide 18
85. Staining a Slide 18
86. Measuring and Counting Using a Microscope 18
87. Calculating Linear Magnification 18
88. Electron Microscopes 18
89. Cell Division 18
90. Mitosis and the Cell Cycle 18
91. Recognising Stages in Mitosis 19
92. Regulation of the Cell Cycle 19
93. Cancer: Cells out of Control 19
94. Binary Fission 19
95. Replication in Viruses 19
96. The Role of Membranes in Cells 19
97. The Structure of Membranes 19
98. How Do We Know? Membrane Structure 20
99. Factors Altering Membrane Permeability 20
100. Diffusion 20
101. Osmosis 20
102. Water Movement in Plant Cells 20
103. Making Dilutions 21
104. Estimating Osmolarity 21
105. Active Transport 21

CONTENTS AQA BIOLOGY 1

106	Ion Pumps	21
107	Exocytosis and Endocytosis	22
108	Cell Recognition	22
109	The Body's Defences	22
110	Antigenic Variability	22
111	The Action of Phagocytes	22
112	The Immune System	22
113	Clonal Selection	22
114	Antibodies	22
115	Acquired Immunity	22
116	Vaccines and Vaccination	23
117	Questions About Vaccines	23
118	HIV/AIDS	23
119	Monoclonal Antibodies	23
120	Herceptin: A Modern Monoclonal	24
121	Chapter Review	24
122	KEY TERMS: Did You Get It?	24

Organisms exchange substances with their environment

123	Limitations to Cell Size	24
124	Introduction to Gas Exchange	24
125	Gas Exchange in Animals	24
126	Gas Exchange in Insects	24
127	Gas Exchange in Fish	25
128	Gas Exchange in Plants	25
129	Adaptations of Xerophytes	25
130	The Human Gas Exchange System	25
131	Breathing in Humans	25
132	Measuring Lung Function	26
133	Measuring Vital Capacity	26
134	Respiratory Disease	26
135	Risk Factors for Lung Disease	26
136	Reducing the Risk of Lung Disease	26
137	The Role of the Digestive System	26
138	Digestion	27
139	Optimal pH of Digestive Enzymes	27
140	Absorption	27
141	Transport and Exchange in Animals	27
142	Circulatory Fluids	27
143	Haemoglobins	27
144	Gas Transport in Humans	28
145	The Mammalian Transport System	28
146	Arteries	28
147	Veins	28
148	Capillaries	28
149	Capillary Networks	28
150	The Formation of Tissue Fluid	28
151	The Human Heart	29
152	The Cardiac Cycle	29
153	Dissection of a Mammalian Heart	29
154	Exercise and Heart Rate	29
155	Cardiovascular Disease	29
156	CVD Risk Factors	30
157	Reducing the Risk	30
158	Evaluating the Risk	30
159	Vascular Tissue in Plants	30
160	Xylem and Phloem	30
161	Identifying Xylem and Phloem	30
162	Uptake at the Root	30
163	Transpiration	30
164	Investigating Plant Transpiration	31
165	Translocation	31
166	Experimental Evidence for Plant Transport	31
167	Chapter Review	31
168	KEY TERMS: Did You Get It?	31

Genetic information, variation, and relationships between organisms

169	Prokaryotic Chromosome Structure	32
170	Eukaryotic Chromosome Structure	32
171	Genomes	32
172	The Genetic Code	32
173	DNA Carries the Code	32
174	Genes to Proteins	33
175	Transcription in Eukaryotes	33
176	Translation	33
177	Protein Synthesis Summary	33
178	Gene Mutations and Mutagens	33
179	Meiosis	33
180	Crossing Over Problems	34
181	Modelling Meiosis	34
182	Mitosis vs Meiosis	34
183	Non-Disjunction In Meiosis	34
184	Meiosis and Life Cycles	34
185	The Mechanism of Natural Selection	34
186	Types of Natural Selection	34
187	The Evolution of Antibiotic Resistance	35
188	Measuring Antibiotic Sensitivity	35
189	Selection for Human Birth Weightt	35
190	Observing Natural Selection	35
191	Adaptation and Fitness	36
192	The Biological Species Concept	36
193	The Phylogenetic Species Concept	36
194	Behaviour and Species Recognition	36
195	Classification Systems	36
196	Biodiversity	37
197	Sampling Populations	37
198	Interpreting Samples	37
199	Diversity Indices	37
200	Investigating Biodiversity	37
201	Agriculture and Biodiversity	38
202	Hedgerows	38
203	Quantifying Variation Using Student's t-Test	38
204	Quantitative Investigation of Variation	39
205	Investigating Genetic Diversity	39
206	Homologous DNA Sequences	39
207	Homologous Proteins	39
208	Genetic Diversity in Springtails	39
209	Genetic Biodiversity in Endangered Populations	40
210	Chapter Review	40
211	KEY TERMS: Did You Get It?	40

1. How Do We Do Science? (page 5)
1. Citations support the statements made in the text and show you have researched the topic. Referencing helps identify the sources of the citation for validation and for future checking.
2. Student's own response, but should reflect that science is not a linear process and ideas can change with the acquisition of new knowledge.

2. Hypotheses and Predictions (page 6)
1. (a) There are several hypotheses that could be generated to explain these observations:
    - Bright colour patterns might signal to potential predators that the caterpillars are distasteful.
    - Inconspicuous caterpillars are good to eat and their cryptic colouration reduces the chance that they will be discovered and eaten.
   (b) Null forms of these hypotheses:
    - There is no difference in palatability between the bright and cryptically coloured caterpillars.
    - There is no difference between the cryptic and brightly coloured caterpillars in the ease with which they are detected by predators.
   (c) Possible assumptions:
    - Birds and other predators have colour vision.
    - Birds and other predators can learn about the palatability of their prey by tasting them.
   (d) Prediction 1: That birds will avoid preying on brightly coloured, conspicuous caterpillars.
   Prediction 2: Naive (inexperienced) birds will learn from a distasteful experience with an unpalatable caterpillar species and will avoid them thereafter.
   Prediction 3: Birds will prey readily on cryptically coloured caterpillars if these are provided as food.

3. Types of Data (page 7)
1. (a) Skin colour: ranked data.
   (b) Number of eggs: quantitative data, discontinuous.
   (c) Tree trunk diameter: quantitative data, continuous.
2. Quantitative data are more easily analysed in a meaningful way, e.g. by using descriptive statistics.
3. Examples include: gender, viability (dead or alive), species, presence or absence of a feature, flower colour. These data are categorical; no numerical value can be assigned to them.
4. The students should express the abundance of plant species quantitatively, e.g. as percentage cover of a specific species or the number of individual plants present.

4. Making a Qualitative Investigation (page 8)
1. (a) All samples had to be heated for the same amount of time to ensure they all received the same treatment conditions for reaction.
   (b) Stirring ensures maximum contact of substrate and enzyme therefore maximising reaction.
2. As the bananas ripen, the starch is converted to simple sugars fructose and glucose.
3. (a) Fructose is a ketose sugar, but it is converted to glucose in the basic reagent and the aldehyde group gives a positive test.
   (b) You cannot tell from the test results if the banana ripening resulted in conversion of starch to glucose alone or to fructose (fruit sugar) and glucose.

5. Making a Quantitative Investigation (page 9)
1. Aim: To investigate the effect of temperature on the rate of catalase activity.
2. Hypothesis: The rate of catalase activity is dependent on temperature.
3. (a) Independent variable: Temperature.
   (b) 10-60°C in uneven steps: 10°C, 20°C, 30°C, 60°C.
   (c) Unit: °C
   (d) Equipment: A means to maintain the test-tubes at the set temperatures, e.g. water baths. Equilibrate all reactants to the required temperatures in each case, before adding enzyme to the reaction tubes.
4. (a) Dependent variable: Height of oxygen bubbles.
   (b) Unit: mm
   (c) Equipment: Ruler; place vertically alongside the tube and read off the height (directly facing).
5. (a) Each temperature represents a treatment.
   (b) No. of tubes at each temperature = 2
   (c) Sample size: for each treatment = 2
   (d) Times the investigation repeated = 3
6. Tubes 9 and 10 are the controls.
7. Controlled variables (a-c in any order):
   (a) **Catalase and H_2O_2 from the same batch source and with the same storage history**. Storage and batch history can be determined.
   (b) **Equipment of the same type and size** (i.e. using test-tubes of the same dimensions, as well as volume). This could be checked before starting.
   (c) **Same person doing the measurements of height each time**. This should be decided beforehand.
   Note that some variables were controlled: The test-tube volume, and the volume of each reactant. Control of measurement error is probably the most important after these considerations.

6. Accuracy and Precision (page 11)
1. Accuracy refers to the correctness of the measurement, or how close a measurement is to the true value. Precision refers to the repeatability of the measurements (how close the measured values are to each other).
2. (a) 6   (d) 5
   (b) 2   (e) 6
   (c) 1   (f) 2

7. Working With Numbers (page 12)
1. 5600 mm^3
2. 43 000 i.e. 43 x 1000
3. 15 i.e. 3 x 70 = 210 ÷ 10 = 21.
   210 ÷ 20 = 10.5 and 15 is halfway between 21 and 10.5
4. 33, i.e. 66 ÷ 2
5. 45 000 + 645 000
6. 690 000
7. 6.9 x 10^5

8. Fractions, Percentages, and Ratios (page 13)
1. (a) 28 : 14 : 3: 2: 1 Divide all values by 5
   (b) Interphase = 2800
   Prophase = 1400
   Telophase = 300
   Metaphase = 200
   Anaphase = 100
2. (a) 1/3   (b) 14/15   (c) 1/11
3. 1/3
   (5/20 x 6 = 30/120) + (5/12 x 10 = 50/120) = 2/3. 2/3 ÷ 2 = 1/3.
4. % lean body mass
   Athlete: 76.0%
   Lean: 73.2%
   Normal weight 70.8%
   Overweight 60.0%
   Obese 54.7%

9. Logs and Exponents (page 14)
1. As body mass increases, basal metabolic rate decreases.
2. In power functions, the base value is variable and the exponent is fixed. In exponential functions the base value is fixed and the exponent is variable.

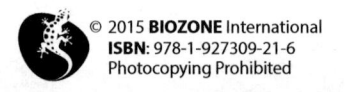

3. (a) A log transformation is used in data that is increasing exponentially.
   (b) Log transformations normalise data and make large numbers easier to work with.

10. Properties of Geometric Shapes (page 15)
1. (a) 12.5 cm   (b) 50.2 cm^2 (c) 33.5 cm^3
2. (a) 15 mm^2 (b) 1.8 cm^3
3. (a) 489.5 cm^2 (b) 829.7 cm^3
4. 48 = l x w x h
   8 = 4 x 2.5 x h
   h = 48/10 = 4.8
5. 27 = $\pi r^2 h$ = $\pi r^2 \times 3$
   27/3 = πr^2
   27/3π = r^2
   $\sqrt{27/3\pi}$ = r
   r = 1.69
6. (a) SA = $4\pi r^2$ = $4\pi \times 0.2^2$ = 0.50 μm^2
   (b) V = 4/3 x πr^3 = 4/3 x π x 0.2^3 = 0.033 μm^3
   (c) 80% of 0.2 = 0.16. SA = $4\pi r^2$ = $4\pi \times 0.16^2$ = 0.32 μm
   (d) V = 4/3 x πr^3 = 4/3 x π x 0.16^3 = 0.017 μm^3
   (e) Original cell 0.5/0.033 = 15.1 = 15:1
       New cell 0.32/0.017 - 18.8 = 19:1

11. Practising With Data (page 16)
1. Performing data transformations:
   (a) Photosynthetic rate at different light intensities:

Light intensity	Average time (min)	Reciprocal of time (min^{-1})
100	15	0.067
50	25	0.040
25	50	0.020
11	93	0.011
6	187	0.005

(b) Water loss with bubble potometer

Time	Pipette arm reading (cm^3)	Plant water loss (cm^3 min^{-1})
0	9.0	-
5	8.0	0.2
10	7.2	0.16
15	6.2	0.2
20	4.9	0.26

(c) Incidence of cyanogenic clover in different regions:

Clover type	Frost free No.	%	Frost prone No.	%	Totals
Cyanogenic	124	78	26	18	150
Acyanogenic	35	22	115	82	150
Total	159	100	141	100	300

(d) Frequency of size classes of eels:

Size class (mm)	Frequency	Relative frequency (%)
0-50	7	2.6
50-99	23	8.5
100-149	59	21.9
150-199	98	36.3
200-249	50	18.5
250-299	30	11.1
300-349	3	1.1
Total	270	100.0

2. (a) 8.970 x 10^3 (b) 4.6 x 10^{-2} (c) 1.467851 x 10^6
3. (a) 0.43   (b) 0.000031   (c) 62 000
4. (a)

Chilli Beans Nutrition Facts Serving size 1 cup (253 g)		
Amount per serving		% Composition
Total Fat	8 g	3.2
– Saturated Fat	3 g	1.2
Total Carbohydrate	22 g	8.7
– Dietary Fibre	9 g	3.5
– Sugars	4 g	1.6
Protein	25 g	9.9

(b) Dietary fibre 3.5%   Sugars: 1.6%
(c) 72%

12. Apparatus and Measurement (page 17)
1. (a) 25 mL graduated cylinder
   (b) 50 mL graduated cylinder
   (c) 10 mL pipette
2. (a) ((0.98-1)/1) x 100 = -2%
   (b) ((9.98-10/10) x 100 = -0.2%
   (c) The greater the sample value the lower the percentage error when the error value remains constant.

13. Recording Results (page 18)
1. See table below.
2. The table would be three times as big in the vertical dimension; the layout of the top of the table would be unchanged. The increased vertical height of the table would accommodate the different ranges of the independent variable (full light, as in question 1, but also half light, and low light). These ranges would have measured values attached to them (they should be quantified, rather than subjective values).

14. Constructing Tables and Graphs (page 19)
1. The two means are not significantly different because the 95% CIs overlap. The mean at 4 gm^{-3} has such a large 95% CI we cannot be confident that it is significantly different from the mean at 3 gm^{-3}.

		Trial 1 [CO$_2$] in ppm (day 0)										Trial 2 [CO$_2$] in ppm (day 2)										Trial 3 [CO$_2$] in ppm (day 4)									
		Minutes										Minutes										Minutes									
	Set up no.	0	1	2	3	4	5	6	7	8	9	10	0	1	2	3	4	5	6	7	8	9	10	0	1	2	3	4	5	6	7	8	9	10
Full light conditions	1																																		
	2																																		
	3																																		
	Mean																																		

© 2015 BIOZONE International
ISBN: 978-1-927309-21-6
Photocopying Prohibited

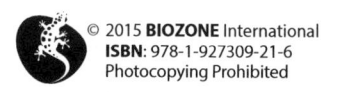

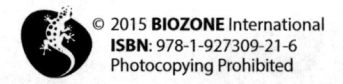

MODEL ANSWERS AQA BIOLOGY 1

2. Graphs and tables provide different ways of presenting information. Tables summarise raw data, provide an accurate record of the data values, and can record summary statistics. Graphs present information in a way that make trends and relationships in the data apparent. Both are valuable.

16. Drawing Bar Graphs (page 21)
1. (a)

Species	Site 1	Site 2
Ornate limpet	21	30
Radiate limpet	6	34
Limpet sp. A	38	-
Limpet sp. B	57	39
Limpet sp. C	-	2
Catseye	6	2
Topshell	2	4
Chiton	1	3

Bar graph: Average abundance of eight mollusc species at two sites along a rocky shore

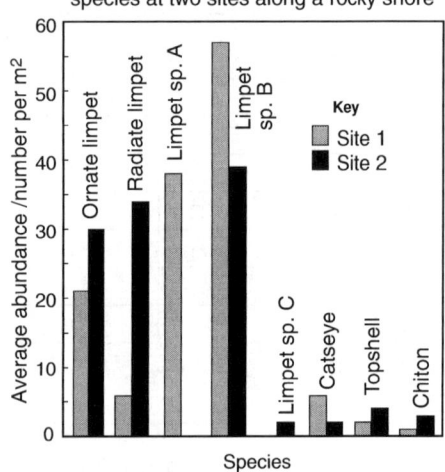

17. Drawing Histograms (page 22)
1. (a)

Weight / kg	Total	Weight / kg	Total
45-49.9	1	80-84.9	16
50-54.9	2	85-89.9	9
55-59.9	7	90-94.9	5
60-64.9	13	95-99.9	2
65-69.9	15	100-104.9	0
70-74.9	13	105-109.9	1
75-79.9	11		

(b) *Frequency histogram of weights of 95 individuals (males and females)*

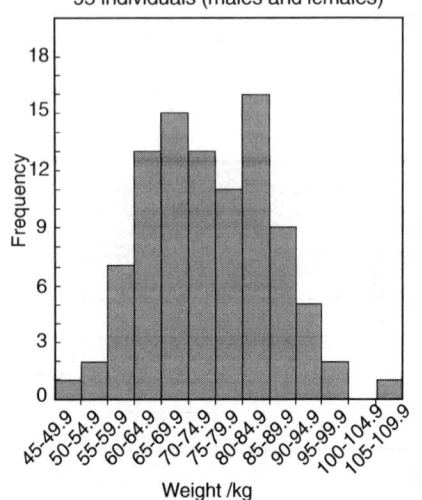

18. Drawing Line Graphs (page 23)
1. (a) *Rate of reaction of enzyme A at different temperatures*

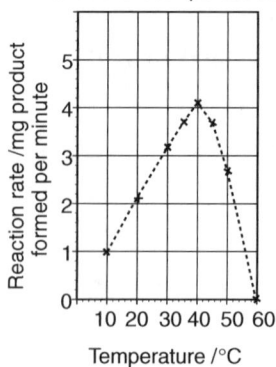

(b) Rate of reaction at 15°C = 1.6 mg product min^{-1}

2. (a) Line graph and (b) point at which shags and nests were removed: See graph top of next page.

19. Correlation or Causation (page 25)
1. A correlation between variables does not mean that one variable causes or is even related to the other.

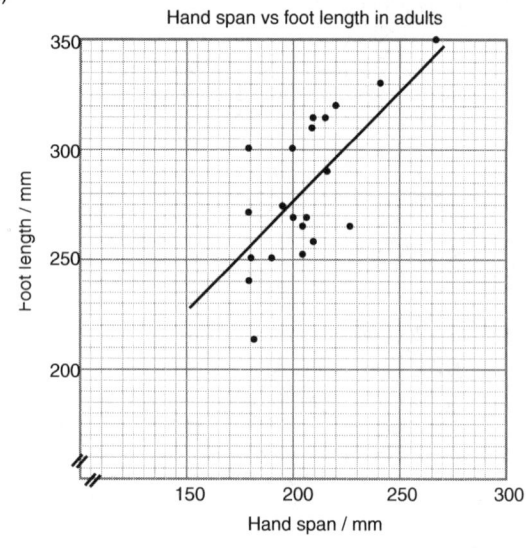

2. (a) *Hand span vs foot length in adults*

(b) There is a general trend in that a larger hand span will have a longer foot length.
(c) There is a positive relationship between hand span and foot length but it is not very strong. (r^2 = 0.5 calc. in Excel)

20. Drawing Scatter Plots (page 26)
1. (a) and (b): Scatter plot and fitted curve:

Oxygen consumption of fish with affected gills

© 2015 BIOZONE International
ISBN: 978-1-927309-21-6
Photocopying Prohibited

AQA BIOLOGY 1 MODEL ANSWERS

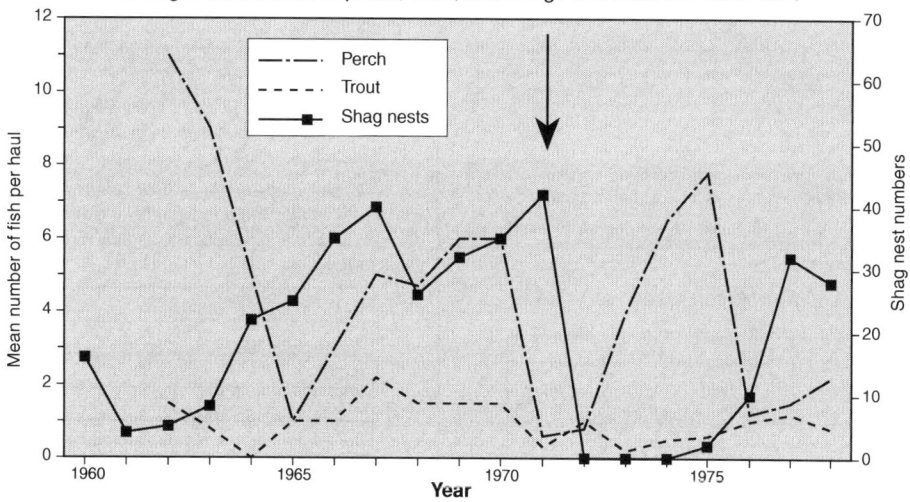

Changes in numbers of perch, trout, and shags in a reservoir 1960-1978

2. (a) **At rest**: No clear relationship. The line on the graph appears to have no significant slope and although here is a slight tendency for oxygen consumption to fall as more of the gill becomes affected, the scatter makes this relationship inconclusive.
    (b) **Swimming**: A negative linear relationship; the greater the proportion of affected gill, the lower the oxygen consumption.
3. The gill disease appears to have little or no effect on the oxygen uptake in resting fish.

21. Interpreting Line Graphs (page 27)
1. (a) 2 (2:1) (b) -1 (c) 0
2. (a) 2 (b) 14
3. (a) 1 (b) 2
   (c) 5 (d) Positive straight

23. Spearman Rank Correlation (page 29)
Missing values completed at the top of the column:
1. There is no correlation between the volume of a male frigatebird's throat pouch and the frequency (pitch) of the drumming sound made.
2. (a) 0.59
   (b) Negative
   (c) Not significant

Bird	Rank (R_1)	Rank (R_2)	Difference (D) (R_1-R_2)	D^2
1	2	3	-1	1
2	1	6	-5	25
3	4	12	-8	64
4	5	4	-1	1
5	3	8.5	-3.5	12.25
6	7	10	-3	9
7	6	11	-5	25
8	9	7	2	4
9	8	8.5	-0.5	0.25
10	10.5	1	9.5	90.25
11	10.5	5	5.5	30.25
12	12	2	10	100
		Σ(Sum)	0	362

r_s value = -0.266

3. Class analysis will vary but there is likely a correlation between these both at the individual an class level.

24. Mean, Median, and Mode (page 30)
1. The modal value and associated ranked entries indicate that the variable being measured (swimmers' height) has a bimodal distribution; the data are not normally distributed. Therefore the mean and median are not accurate indicators of central tendency.
   Note: the median differs from the mean; also an indication of a skewed (non-normal) distribution.
2. The modal value and associated ranked entries indicate that the variable being measured (sori per frond) has a bimodal distribution i.e. the data are not normally distributed. Therefore the mean and median are not accurate indicators of central tendency. Note also that the median differs from the mean; also an indication of a skewed (non-normal) distribution.
3.

Ladybird mass (mg)	Tally	Total
6.2	I	1
6.7	I	1
7.7	II	2
7.8	I	1
8.0	I	1
8.2	I	1
8.4	I	1
8.8	IIII	4
8.9	I	1
9.8	I	1
10.1	I	1

Median = 8th value when in rank order = 8.4

Mode = 8.8

Mean = 124.7 ÷ 15 = 8.3

Note: To plot a histogram, missing weight classes would have to be included with values of 0.

25. Spread of Data (page 32)
1. The larger standard deviation for the first data set indicates the spread of values around the mean is greater than in the second set. The second data set is likely to be more reliable.
2. (a) 139.31 ÷ 40 = 3.483
   (b) 0.647
   (c) 2.836 - 4.13 (3.483 ± 0.647)
   (d) 75% (30 out of 40)
   (e) It is normally distributed around the mean.

26. Interpreting Sample Variability (page 33)
1. (a) 496/689 values within ± 1sd of the mean = 72% (48±7.8, i.e. between 40.2 and 55.8)
   (b) 671//689 values within ± 2 sd of the mean = 97% (48± 15.6, i.e. between 32.4 and 63.6)
   (c) The data are close to being normally distributed about the mean (normal = 67% of values within 1 sd of mean and 95% of values between 2 sd of mean).
2. The mean and the median are very close.

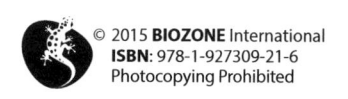

© 2015 **BIOZONE** International
ISBN: 978-1-927309-21-6
Photocopying Prohibited

3. N = 30 data set
   (a) **Mean** = 49.23
   (b) **Median** = 49.5
   (c) **Mode** = 38
   (d) **Sample variance** = 129.22
   (e) **Standard deviation** = 11.37

4. N = 50 data set
   (a) **Mean** = 61.44
   (b) **Median** = 63
   (c) **Mode** = 64
   (d) **Sample variance** = 14.59
   (e) **Standard deviation** = 3.82

5. Frequency histogram for the N=50 perch data set.

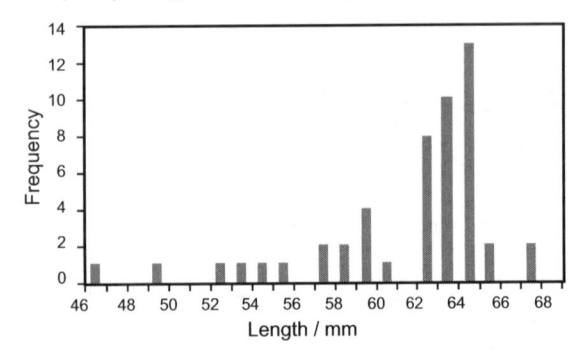

   Frequency histogram for the N = 30 perch data set.

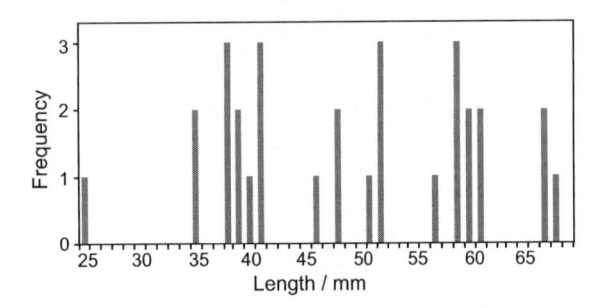

6. (a) The mean and median are very close to each other for the N=30 data set. There is a larger difference between the mean and median values obtained in the N=50 data set.
   (b) The standard deviation obtained for the N=30 set is much larger (11.37) compared to only 3.82 for the larger N=50 data set.
   (c) The N=30 data set more closely resembles the complete data set. The mean and median are quite close to those of the original data set. The mean, median and mode for the N=50 data set are considerably higher than those statistics for the complete data set. The sample variance and standard deviation values for the complete data set fall between those of the two smaller data sets.

7. (a) Histogram for the N=30 data set shows a relatively normal distribution of data. Histogram for the N=50 data set shows a non-normal distribution which is skewed to the right (negative skew).
   (b) The person who collected the sample in the N=30 data set used equipment and techniques designed to collect fish randomly. As a result, a normal distribution of fish sizes was obtained by their sampling methods. Fish collection for the N=50 sample set was biased. The mesh size used did not retain smaller fish, so a larger proportion of bigger fish were collected. When plotted on a frequency histogram the data presented as a negative skew.

28. Practising Biological Drawings (page 37)

1. Student's own work. Red blood cells are the most numerous. Neutrophils should be the most numerous white blood cells.

29. Test Your Understanding (page 38)

1. Fertiliser concentration.
   Range: 0.0-0.30 g dm^{-3} in steps of 0.06 g dm^{-3}.

2. 5

3. Outlying value = 23.6. This value should not be used in calculations as it is likely it is an anomalous event and could skew the result.

4. Missing values below. For treatment 0.24 g dm^{-3} values are with outlier included (without outlier):

Fertiliser concn	Total mass	Mean mass
0.0	408.5	81.7
0.06	546.3	109.3
0.12	591.4	118.28
0.18	510.1	127.5
0.24	582.5 (558.9)	116.5 (139.7)
0.30	610.4	122.1

5. Completed graph below. Only the plot with outlier excluded is shown.

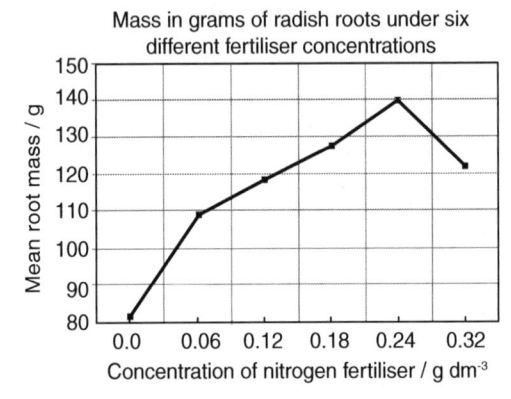

6. The students should have recorded the dry mass of the root, by first drying the root in an oven at low temperature to remove any water.

7. Measuring only the root mass fails to take into account the amount of growth/mass in the leaves.

8. Measuring the mass of the leaves, the number of leaves, the diameter on the root, the length of the root, the length of the leaves etc.

9.
Fertiliser concn	Mean	Median	Mode
0.0	8.6	9	9
0.06	15.6	16	16
0.12	16.6	17	17
0.18	18.2	18	18
0.24	18.5	18.5	No mode
0.30	18.2	18	No mode

10. (a) 6 (0.24 g dm^{-3} sample 1)
    (b) 16
    (c) With outlier 5.02 Without outlier 0.5
    (d) The (biased) mean does not properly reflect the data set when the outlier is included. The standard deviation is vastly increased to accommodate the outlier while all other values are above the (biased) mean and within only one standard deviation.

11. 0.24 g dm^{-3} fertiliser (after removing the outlier).

12. Not all plants in sample may have received the same amount of fertiliser/water. Plants in centre of group may be more shaded/protected.

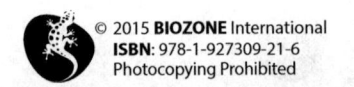

AQA BIOLOGY 1 MODEL **ANSWERS**

13. Nitrogen fertiliser increases the growth of radish plants, but only up to a limit, with peak performance reached at 0.24 g dm^{-3} of fertiliser. The fertiliser also increases the number of leaves per plant (up to a limit) which is likely related to the overall increase in growth of the plant.

14. Replication decreases the likelihood of chance events affecting results or may identify true results that may have been attributed to chance. It helps to remove uncontrollable factors and adds weight to the findings.

30. Organic Molecules (page 43)
1. Carbon, hydrogen, and oxygen.
2. Sulfur and nitrogen.
3. (a) Arrows should indicate the four electrons in the outer shell.
   (b) Four covalent bonds (valency of 4).
4. A molecular (or chemical) formula shows the numbers and kinds of atoms in a molecule whereas a structural formula is the graphical representation of the molecular structure showing how the atoms are arranged.

31. The Biochemical Nature of Cells (page 44)
1. A monomer is a repeated component of a larger organic molecule. A polymer is an organic molecule made up a repeated monomers.
2. (a) Carbohydrates: A major structural component of most plant cells, a ready source of energy, and they are involved in cellular recognition. Can be converted to fats.
   (b) Lipids: A ready store of energy (their energy yield per gram is twice that of carbohydrates). They also provide insulation and transport fat-soluble vitamins. Phospholipids are a major component of cellular membranes.
   (c) Proteins: Required for growth and repair of cells and tissues. Roles in catalysing reactions, cell signalling, internal defence, contraction, and transport. Can be converted to fats.
   (d) Nucleic acids, e.g. DNA and RNA, encode the genetic information for the construction and functioning of an organism. Nucleotide derivatives (e.g. ATP) are energy carriers in the cell.

32. The Common Ancestry of Life (page 45)
1. A universal common ancestor is supported by similarities in the molecular machinery of life (e.g. DNA, RNA, ribosomes and other replication machinery) and by the fact that almost all organisms shcare the same genetic code.
2. Mitochondria and chloroplasts have their own DNA (distinct from the nuclear DNA) and the ribosomes in mitochondria and chloroplasts are similar to those in bacteria, supporting a bacterial origin for these organelles.
3. Molecular techniques have allowed the genetic relatedness of organisms to be clarified by directly comparing DNA, RNA, and proteins. For example, analysis of RNA polymerase enzymes indicates an archaean origin for eukaryotes.

33. Sugars (page 46)
1. (a) Primary energy source for cellular metabolism
   (b) Structural units for disaccharides and polysaccharides (energy sources and structural carbohydrates).
2. Glucose is a hexose sugar (6 carbon atoms) while ribose is a pentose sugar (5 carbon atoms).
3. Isomers have the same molecular formula but their atoms are linked in different sequences. For example, α-glucose and β-glucose are isomers because, although they have the same molecular formula ($C_6H_{12}O_6$), they are structurally different. This difference gives them different chemical properties.

34. Condensation and Hydrolysis of Sugars (page 47)
1. Disaccharide sugars are formed by condensation reactions and broken down by hydrolysis. Condensation reactions join two monosaccharide molecules by a glycosidic bond with the release of a water molecule. Hydrolysis reactions use water to split a disaccharide molecule into two. The water molecule provides a hydrogen atom and a hydroxyl group.
2. A - Condensation, product: maltose
   B - Hydrolysis, products: two glucose molecules
3. Lactose

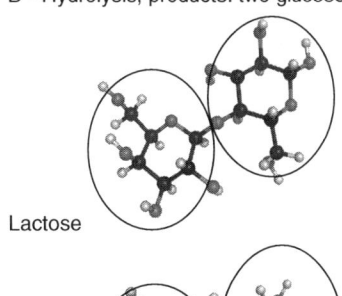

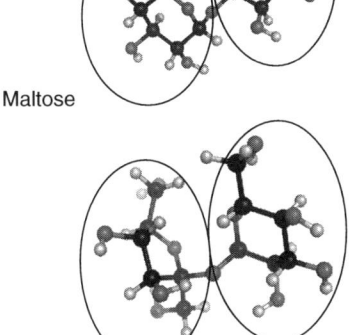

   Maltose

   Sucrose

35. Colorimetry (page 48)
1. (a) Approximately 0.45%
   (b) You would have to dilute the solution so the concentrations fell within the range of the calibration curve.
2. To quantify the glucose concentration of a drink, you would:
   (1) Perform a Benedict's test on each of the commercial drinks.
   (2) Measure and record the absorbance for each sample.
   (3) Determine the glucose concentration of the commercial samples by reading their absorbance off the calibration curve.
   Note: The glucose calibration curve is prepared by measuring the absorbance of a number of known glucose standards.
3. Suspended solids could absorb or refract light, producing an incorrect absorbance for the substance being tested.

36. Polysaccharides (page 49)
1. (a) Polysaccharides are a good source of energy because they are easily hydrolysed into monosaccharides (e.g. glucose) when energy is needed. Monosaccharides are the primary source of cellular fuel.
   (b) Polysaccharides are hydrolysed to produce simpler carbohydrates, e.g. glucose, which can then be transported to other parts of the organism.
2. Glycogen is a highly branched glucose polymer. Its branching makes it compact, more soluble in water than starch, and easily hydrolysed to provide glucose for cellular fuel. Glycogen's properties allow it to be metabolised more quickly, which suits the active lives of moving animals. Starch is a mix of branched and unbranched chains of glucose, which makes it powdery. It is less compact than glycogen, relatively insoluble in cold water, but relatively easy to hydrolyse to soluble sugars, making it a good storage molecule for plants. Cellulose is a linear glucose polymer and is strong and insoluble, which makes it well suited to its role in providing strength and support to plant cells.

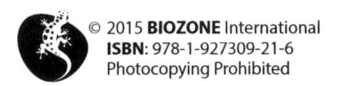

37. Starch and Glucose (page 50)
1. (a) Amyloplasts   (b) The cell wall

2. Amylose is a linear molecule formed from glucose molecules held together by α-1, 4 glycosidic bonds. Amylopectin is similar but it also contains α-1, 6 glycosidic bonds, which provide branching points every 20-30 glucose monomers.

3. Cellulose is a linear molecule consisting of several hundred to several thousand β-glucose molecules bonded by a β -1,4 glycosidic bond. Starch is composed of two main molecules; amylose which forms a helix, and a branched molecule, amylopectin.

4. There are more α-1,6 glycosidic bonds in glycogen.

38. Lipids (page 51)
1. (a) Glycerol
   (b) Ester bond
   (c) Fatty acid

2. Fats need more oxidation per gram to form CO_2 than other molecules and so more usable energy can be extracted from the oxidation reactions.

3. (a) Saturated fatty acids contain the maximum number of hydrogen atoms, whereas unsaturated fatty acids contain some double-bonded carbon atoms.
   (b) Saturated fatty acids tend to produce lipids that are solid at room temperature, whereas lipids that contain a high proportion of unsaturated fatty acids tend to be liquid at room temperature.

4. (a) During esterification, a glycerol molecule is joined with a fatty acid. This occurs three times to form a triglyceride.
   (b) Hydrolysis of a triglyceride produces glycerol and three fatty acids.

5. Key points for required answer underlined: Lipids are a more concentrated source of energy than carbohydrates or proteins, providing fuel for aerobic respiration through fatty acid oxidation. They are important as energy storage molecules, and carbohydrates and protein can both be converted into fats by enzymes and stored within adipose (fat) cells. Fat absorbs shocks and cushions internal organs such as the kidneys and heart. Stored lipids provide insulation and reduce heat loss to the environment. Lipids are a source of metabolic water, e.g. the camel's hump is a store of fat that can be metabolised to provide water as well as energy. As steroids, they are important as hormones (e.g. aldosterone, testosterone) and transport fat soluble vitamins (e.g. vitamin E). Waxes and oils provide waterproofing to the surfaces of organisms and phospholipids form cellular membranes.

39. Phospholipids (page 53)
1. (a) The amphipathic nature of phospholipids (with a polar, hydrophilic end and a hydrophobic, fatty acid end) causes them to orientate in aqueous solutions so that the hydrophobic 'tails' point in together. Hence the bilayer nature of membranes.
   (b) The cellular membranes of an Arctic fish could be expected to contain a higher proportion of unsaturated fatty acids than those of a tropical fish species. This would help them to remain fluid and functional at low temperatures.

2. Unsaturated phospholipids can not pack together as tightly as saturated phospholipids there are more "spaces" within the membrane bilayer, making the membrane more fluid.

40. Amino Acids (page 54)
1. (a) The R group
   (b) The sequence of amino acids in the polypeptide chain.
   (c) The order of nucleotides in DNA and RNA.
   (d) The differences between amino acids are due to the different properties of the R group. These cause different kinds of intermolecular bonding between amino acids in the polypeptide chain, which influences the way the polypeptide will fold up.

2. (a) A peptide bond
   (b) the bond forms by a condensation reaction
   (c)

   $$H_2N-\underset{\underset{H}{|}}{\overset{\overset{R_1}{|}}{C}}-\underset{\underset{H}{|}}{\overset{\overset{O}{\|}}{C}}\ominus\overset{\overset{H}{|}}{N}-\underset{\underset{H}{|}}{\overset{\overset{R_2}{|}}{C}}-\overset{\overset{O}{\|}}{C}\diagdown_{OH}$$

   (d) Di- and polypeptides are broken down by hydrolysis.

41. Chromatography (page 55)
1. Rf = 15 mm ÷ 33 mm = 0.45

2. Rf must always be less than one because the substance cannot move further than the solvent front.

3. Immersion would just wash out the substance into solution instead of separating the components behind a solvent front.

4. (a) A = 0.7   B = 0.5
   (b) A = Alanine   B = Glycine

5. (a) Alanine and arginine
   (b) Their Rf values are very close together.

42. Protein Shape is Related to Function (page 56)
1. The sequence of amino acids (primary structure) determines how a protein folds. The distribution of attractive and repulsive charges on the amino acids determines how the protein is organised and folded (and therefore also determines its biological function).

2. The interior of a plasma membrane is a hydrophobic environment. Channel proteins span the membrane, and fold in such a way that the non-polar (hydrophobic) R-groups align to the outside, and polar (hydrophilic) R-groups form a channel on the inside. This channel allows water soluble molecules to cross the membrane.

3. Denaturation is the process of the protein losing it shape. The loss of shape disrupts the protein's active site and thus its ability to carry out its biological function.

43. Protein Structure (page 57)
1. (a) Peptide bonds between the amino acids.
   (b) α-helices and β-pleated sheets form due to hydrogen bonding.
   (c) Chemical bonds and hydrophobic interactions.
   (d) Interactions between two or more protein molecules or polypeptide chains (subunits).

2. The R groups on each amino acid allow weak intermolecular forces to bind different parts of the polypeptide chain together. This binding causes the polypeptide chain to fold up into the functional shape.

44. Comparing Globular and Fibrous Proteins (page 58)
1. (a) Fibrous proteins, such as collagen and elastin, are part of connective tissues, such as tendons and ligaments (and also in skin), which provide support and rigidity to more fluid components of tissues.
   (b) Enzymes are involved in almost all metabolic reactions. Examples include RuBisCo (photosynthesis), lipase (fat digestion), pyruvate dehydrogenase (cellular respiration).

2. Their tertiary structure produces long fibres or sheets, with many cross-linkages. This makes them very tough physically and ideal as structural molecules.

3. Their tertiary structure produces a globular shape with a specific active site that is critical to their interaction with other molecules and their catalytic activity.

45. Biochemical Tests (page 59)

1. Lipids are not soluble in water. Ethanol acts as a non-polar solvent and is able to dissolve lipids, but is also soluble in water. By dissolving the lipids in the alcohol first, they can then form a mixture, or emulsion, with water that will not separate.
2. When the lipid/ethanol solution is added to water, the lipid forms a precipitate and results in a cloudy appearance.
3. The acid hydrolysis splits the non-reducing sugar into its monosaccharides. These can then be analysed with Benedict's solution.
4. They can not be used to determine concentrations or distinguish between different molecules.

46. Enzymes (page 60)

1. (a) The active site is the region where substrate is drawn in and positioned in such a way as to promote the reaction. The properties of the active site are a function of the precise configuration of the amino acid side chains which interact with the substrate.
   (b) The active site is very specific because of how the protein folds up (its tertiary structure). It will normally accept only one type of molecule (the substrate, which has the correct configuration to interact with the active site).
2. Substrate molecules must collide with the active site.
3. (a) Large molecules are often too big to enter the cell and must be broken down to smaller molecules.
   (b) Extracellular enzymes, such as trypsin, could damage internal proteins if produced in an active form.

47. How Enzymes Work (page 61)

1. Enzymes are biological molecules (usually proteins) that act as catalysts, allowing reactions to proceed more readily. They do this by influencing bond stability in the reactants and thereby lowering the activation energy required to create an unstable transition state in the substrate from which the reaction proceeds readily.
2. A catabolic reaction breaks down complex molecules and releases energy. An anabolic reaction builds complex molecules from simpler ones and involves energy expenditure.

48. Models of Enzyme Activity (page 62)

1. The induced fit model is a modified version of the lock and key in which the substrate and the active site actively interact. The substrate enters the active site and its binding causes a change in the active site so that bonds in the substrate(s) are destabilised.
2. Evidence from studies of enzyme inhibition shows substrate binding causes the active site to change slightly so that bonds in the substrate(s) are destabilised. In light of this evidence the induced fit model has superseded the lock and key model of enzyme action.

49. Enzyme Kinetics (page 63)

1. $(2.4 - 1.4) \div 130 - 72 = 0.017$ cm^3s^{-1}
2. (a) Approximate numbers given. $(3.5 - 2.5) \div (125 - 50) = 0.013$ cm^3s^{-1}
   (b) $(2.5 - 1) \div (50 - 10) = 0.0375$ cm^3s^{-1}
3. (a) Reactants would need to be constantly added to the mix.
   (b) The reactants are being used up.
4. (a) If the substrate is not limited, the reaction rate will increase as the concentration of enzyme is increased.
   (b) A cell may increase the rate of protein synthesis (transcription and translation) to increase the amount of enzyme present, or inactivate enzymes (e.g. by feedback inhibition) to reduce their activity.
5. The rate changes (levels off) because, after a certain concentration of substrate, the enzymes are saturated by the substrate and the reaction rate cannot increase.
6. (a) An optimum temperature for an enzyme is the temperature where enzyme activity is maximal.
   (b) Most enzymes perform poorly at low temperatures because chemical reactions occur slowly or not at all at low temperatures (enzyme activity will reappear when the temperature increases; usually enzymes are not damaged by low temperatures).
   (c) Reaction rate at T°C = $2.4 \div 30 = 0.08$ cm^3s^{-1}
   Reaction rate at T + 10°C = $4 \div 27 = 0.15$ cm^3s^{-1}
   $Q_{10} = 1.88$
7. (a) Optimum pH: pepsin: 1-2, trypsin: approx. 7.5-8.2, urease: approx. 6.5-7.0.
   (b) The stomach is an acidic environment which is the ideal pH for pepsin, whereas trypsin works in the alkaline environment of the small intestine. The optimal pH of urease suits a neutral environment (it is found in soil and bacteria and fungi).

50. Investigating Enzyme Reaction Rates (page 65)

1.

Mass /	Volume O_2 / cm^3			Mean	Rate
	Test 1	Test 2	Test 3		
1	6	5	6	5.7	1.14
2	10	9	9	9.3	1.86
3	14	15	15	14.7	2.94
4	21	20	20	20.3	4.06
5	24	23	25	24	4.8

2. Mass of potato vs rate of gas production

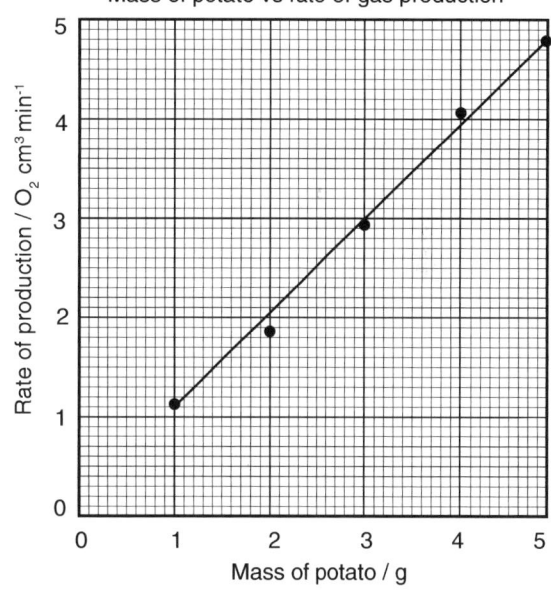

3. The rate of reaction increases with increasing enzyme present.
4. So that the H_2O_2 was not a limiting factor in the reaction.
5. The students should have used a control, that being a flask without potato added to the H_2O_2.
6. (a) There would be no gas evolved.
   (b) Cooking the potato denatures the catalase enzyme.

51. Enzyme Inhibitors (page 66)

1. In **competitive inhibition**, the inhibitor competes with the substrate for the enzyme's active site and, once in place, prevents substrate binding. A **noncompetitive inhibitor** does not occupy the active site but binds to some other part of the enzyme, making it less able to perform its function as an effective biological catalyst.
2. (a) With a competitive inhibitor present, the effect of the

competition can be overcome by increasing the substrate concentration; the rate of the reaction will slow, but will eventually reach the same level as that achieved without an inhibitor. In a system where there is a non-competitive inhibitor, the rate of the reaction slows and is well below the maximum that can be achieved without an inhibitor. This rate depression cannot be overcome by increasing the substrate concentration.

(b) Type of inhibition could be tested by increasing the substrate concentration. If this overcame the rate depression then the inhibition is competitive.

52. Investigating Catalase Activity (page 67)

1. $2H_2O_2 \rightarrow 2H_2O + O_2$

2. (a)-(c), mean, standard deviation, and mean rate below.

Stage	Mean	Std Dev	Mean rate ($cm^3\ s^{-1}\ g^{-1}$)
0.5	10.1	0.5	0.03
2	34.9	3.8	0.12
4	65.5	5.0	0.22
6	36.7	4.0	0.12
10	22.5	2.7	0.08

3. (a) The values obtained for the 0.5 days and 10 days of germination are not in accordance with those obtained by the other groups (trials). The other values are of a similar magnitude.
   (b) If the new data are used, the mean should exclude those two values and be calculated using only 5 (rather than 6) trials for those germination stages.
   (c) These data values are clearly well adrift from the other values obtained for those stages from other groups (trial); if plotted as a scatter plot, they are distinct outliers on the plot. This suggests that something was wrong with either the measurement or the execution of the trial. It is reasonable therefore to exclude them from the analysis.

4. Catalase activity in relation to stage of germination in mung bean seedlings

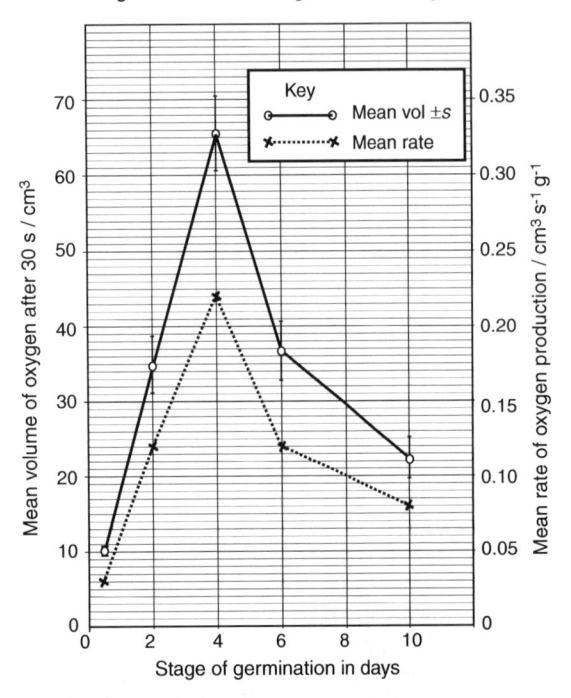

   [Graph: Mean volume of oxygen after 30 s / cm^3 and Mean rate of oxygen production / $cm^3\ s^{-1}\ g^{-1}$ vs Stage of germination in days. Key: Mean vol ±s, Mean rate]

5. (a) The volume and rate of oxygen production increases rapidly to a peak at 4 days and declines, almost as sharply between 4 and 10 days.
   (b) Catalase activity in the sprouting seeds increases rapidly in the first 4 days of germination linked to the increase in cell activity and high respiration rates in early growth. It then falls off as the seedlings become established and metabolism slows.
   (c) In part but the fall off in activity was not predicted.

6. Errors include: The equipment could leak around the bung or the tubing. There could be a delay in delivering all the H_2O_2 so a slight delay in correctly timing the start of the reaction. The seeds might not be completely crushed, or crushed to different degrees so that not all the catalase is released.

7. Validity of data could be affected by (two of): insufficient usable data, highly variable data (overlapping data between times), old or poorly stored beans, old or poorly stored H_2O_2, precise, reliable but inaccurate data because of gas losses through the equipment.

53. Nucleotides (page 69)

1. (a) A, T, C, G   (b) A, U, C, G
2. (a) Deoxyribose   (b) Ribose
3. The nucleotides (bases) are stored in a specific sequence that is used by the cellular machinery to code for amino acids that make protein.

54. Nucleic Acids (page 70)

1. [Diagram of DNA double helix showing 5' and 3' ends, Deoxyribose, H-Bond, Phosphate, Purines and Pyrimidines, with bases T, G, A, C]

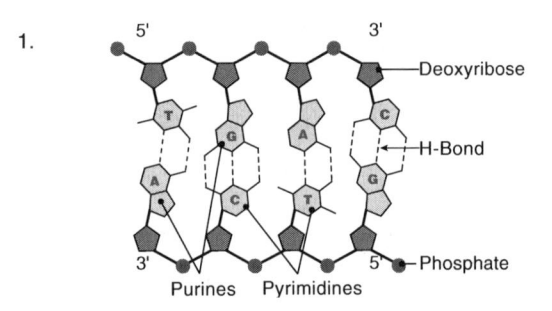

2. (a) The following bases always pair in a normal DS DNA: guanine with cytosine, cytosine with guanine, thymine with adenine, adenine with thymine.
   (b) In mRNA, adenine pairs with uracil (not thymine).
   (c) The hydrogen bonds in double stranded DNA hold the two DNA strands together.

3. mRNAs code for proteins, tRNA moves amino acids to the growing polypeptide chain (to the ribosome binding site), rRNA catalyses formation of a polypeptide.

4. (a) Label uracil or ribose sugar (only found in RNA).
   (b) Label thymine or deoxyribose sugar (only found in DNA).

5. (a) The asymmetric (phosphodiester) bonds in the sugar-phosphate backbone give the molecule a direction so that the two strands in the double-helix run in opposite directions (they are anti-parallel).
   (b) 5' end terminates in a phosphate group, 3' end terminates in a hydroxyl group (from a sugar).

6.
	DNA	RNA
Sugar present	Deoxyribose	Ribose
Bases present	Adenine	Adenine
	Guanine	Guanine
	Cytosine	Cytosine
	Thymine	Uracil
Number of strands	Two (double)	One (single)
Relative length	Long	Short

55. Determining the Structure of DNA (page 72)

1. The gaps in the X shaped pattern. These occurred because of the repeating patten of a double helix.

2. (a) Cellular membranes must be dissolved so that DNA can be removed from the cell.
   (b) Ethanol removes water from around the DNA molecule bringing it out of solution.
   (c) Strawberries have a large number of chromosomes and

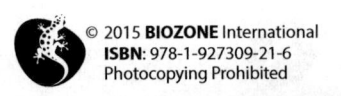

therefore a large amount of DNA in the cell nucleus. This makes it easier to extract a large amount of DNA.

3. Student B's DNA has been cut into short pieces due to the activity of DNase. Student B's extraction mix was probably not cold enough to stop DNase activity.

56. Constructing a DNA Model (page 73)
3. Labels as follows:

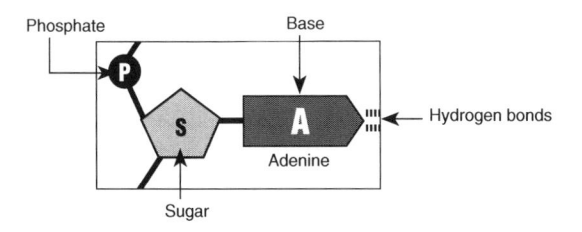

Phosphate, Base, Hydrogen bonds, Adenine, Sugar

4. and 5. below.

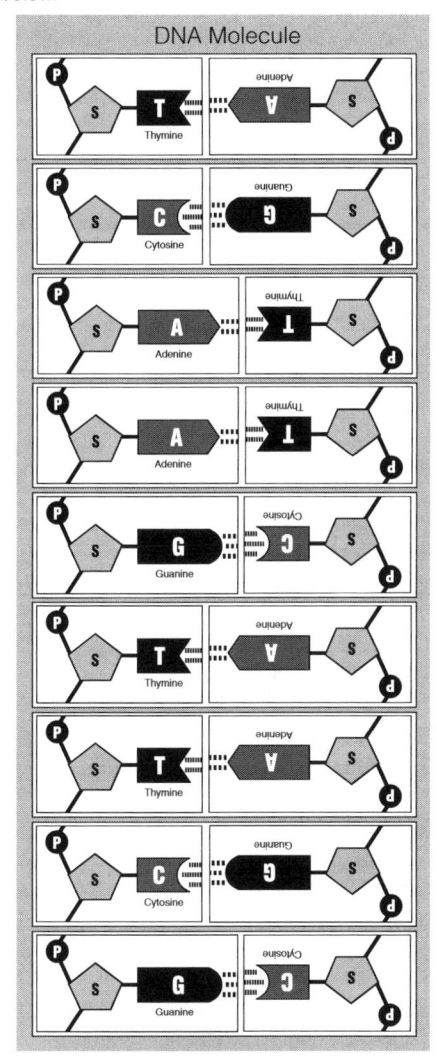

[DNA Molecule diagram showing base pairs: T-A, C-G, A-T, A-T, G-C, T-A, T-A, C-G, G-C]

6. Factors preventing mismatch of nucleotides:
   - The number of hydrogen bond attraction points.
   - The size (length) of the base (thymine and cytosine are short, adenine and guanine are long).
   Examples: Cytosine will not match cytosine because the bases are too far apart, G will not match G because they are too long to fit side by side; T will not match G and C will not match A because there is a mis-match in the number and orientation of H-bonds.

57. DNA Replication (page 77)
1. DNA replication prepares a chromosome for cell division by producing two chromatids which are identical copies of the genetic information for the chromosome.

2. (a) Step 1: Enzymes unwind DNA molecule to expose the two original strands.
   (b) Step 2: DNA polymerase enzyme uses the two original strands as template to make complementary strands.
   (c) Step 3: The two resulting double-helix molecules coil up to form two chromatids.

3. 44

4. 50% new 50% original

5. It means that each new double strand has one strand that is original (parent) DNA.

6. Nucleotides are added to the 3' end of the new DNA strand, matching bases on the parent DNA with complementary bases on the new DNA strand.

7. The base pairing rule ensures that the correct complementary nucleotides on the new DNA are paired with the bases on the parent stand, producing an identical copy of the original DNA.

8. One strand of DNA can only be copied in short segments because the enzymes can only work in the 5' to 3' direction. DNA must be unzipped a short distance before enzymes can begin copying, and they copy in the opposite direction to which the DNA is unzipped.

9. DNA replication is the process by which the DNA molecule is copied to produce two identical DNA strands. Replication is tightly controlled by enzymes. The enzymes also proofread the DNA during replication to correct any mistakes. DNA replication is required before mitosis can occur. After replication, the chromosome is made up of two chromatids. Each chromatid contains half original and half new DNA. The chromatids separate during mitosis.

58. Enzyme Control of DNA Replication (page 79)
1. Enzymes catalyse the reactions that occur during DNA replication. They unwind the DNA, copy the DNA strands, rejoin DNA sequences, and proofread the DNA to correct mistakes. Enzymes are important in ensuring the same sequence of DNA in the parent cell occurs in the daughter cells so that the cell functions normally.

2. (a) **Helicase**: Unwinds the 'parental' strands.
   (b) **DNA polymerase I**: Hydrolyses the RNA primer and replaces it with DNA.
   (c) **DNA polymerase III**: Elongates the leading strand. It synthesises the new Okazaki fragment until it encounters the primer on the previous fragment.
   (d) **Ligase**: Joins Okazaki fragments into a continuous length of DNA.

3. 16 minutes 40 seconds

4. 6 billion x 2 = 12 billion nucleotides. 12 billion ÷ 100 000 = 120 000 mistakes per cell (many are repaired).

59. Meselson and Stahl's Experiment (page 80)
1. (a) Conservative: The original DNA serves as a complete template with the replicated DNA consisting of two completely DNA new strands.
   (b) Semi-conservative: Each DNA strand acts as a template with each replicated DNA consisting of one original strand and one newly replicated strand.
   (c) Dispersive: The replicated DNA strands have old and new DNA scattered throughout them.

2. E. coli were grown in an ^{15}N solution to ensure that the nitrogen atoms in their DNA were all ^{15}N. This allows the DNA of the first generation to be distinguished from the DNA of subsequent generations once they have been transferred back into a ^{14}N solution.

60. Modelling DNA Replication (page 81)

Conservative:

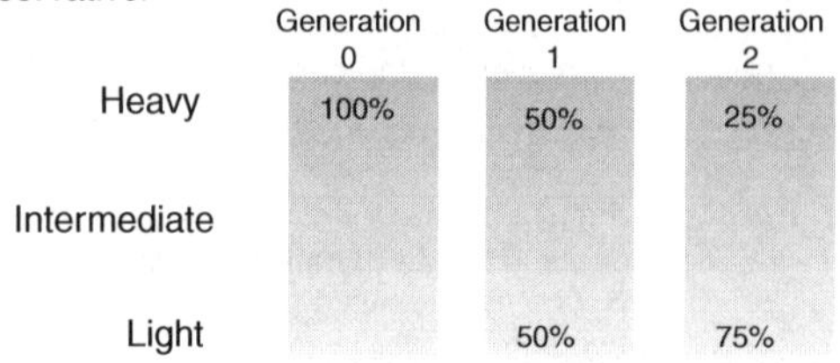

	Generation 0	Generation 1	Generation 2
Heavy	100%	50%	25%
Intermediate			
Light		50%	75%

Semi-conservative:

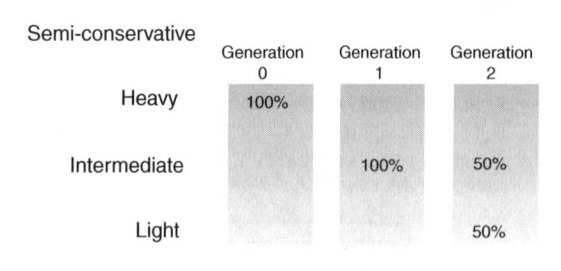

	Generation 0	Generation 1	Generation 2
Heavy	100%		
Intermediate		100%	50%
Light			50%

Dispersive:

	Generation 0	Generation 1	Generation 2
Heavy	100%		
Intermediate		100%	
Light			100%

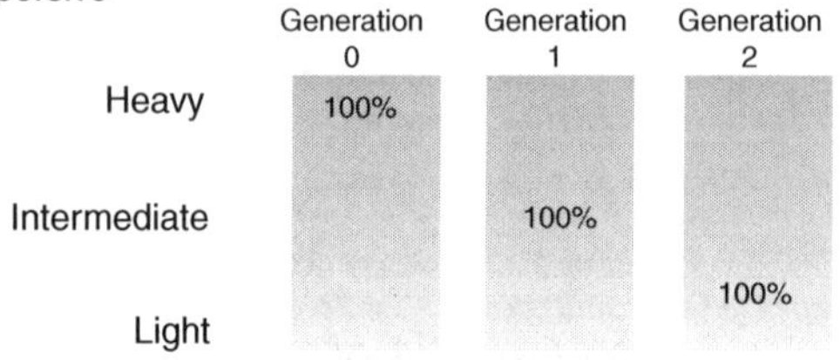

1. (a) Results match the semi-conservative model.
   (b) Yes
2. (a) Conservative   (b) Dispersive

61. ATP: A Nucleotide Derivative (page 84)
1. Mitochondria
2. ATP hydrolase
3. ATP synthase
4. (a) and (b)

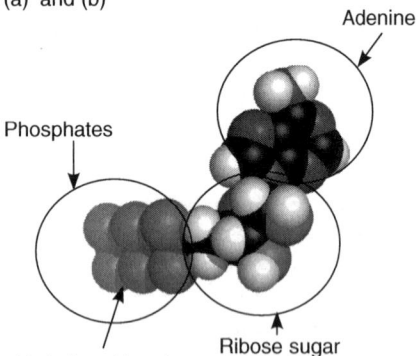

Labels: Adenine, Phosphates, Ribose sugar, Hydrolysed bond

5. Like a rechargeable battery, the ADP/ATP system alternates between a high energy and a low energy state. The addition of a phosphate to ADP recharges the molecule so that it can be used for cellular work.

62. Water (page 85)
1. δ symbol omitted for clarity

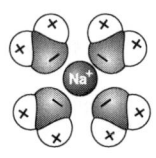

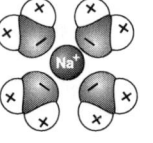

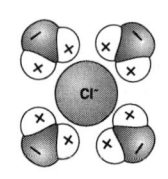

Water surrounding a positive ion (Na^+)
Water surrounding a negative ion (Cl^-)

2. Hydrogen bonds form between hydrogen and a strongly electronegative element such as oxygen. In water, hydrogen bonding helps to hold the water molecules together, making it a stable substance. A relatively large amount of energy is needed to overcome these bonds and separate the water molecules (boiling). A similar bonding occurs between water and other molecules, which makes water a very good solvent.
3. The dipole nature of water allows it form a large number of hydrogen bonds making it a good solvent for many substances, e.g. ionic solids and other polar molecules such as sugars and amino acids. It is therefore readily involved in biochemical reactions.

63. The Properties of Water (page 86)
1. (a) A hydrophobic molecule is not attracted to water whereas a hydrophilic molecule is attracted to water.
   (b) Hydrophilic molecules attract water. Hydrogen or ionic-dipole bonds keep the hydrophilic molecule or ion surrounded by water molecules and keep it dissolved. It thus travels through the blood as a dissolved molecule or ion, e.g. Na^+ or glucose. Hydrophobic molecules will not form intermolecular bonds with water and thus will not dissolve. They must be transported around the body by other methods, often attaching to transport molecules in cells, such as oxygen binding to haemoglobin in the blood.
2. Water absorbs heat energy from the body. The energy breaks the hydrogen bonds between the water molecules and they evaporate. Thus the body feels cooler as heat is transferred from the body to the water in the sweat.

64. Inorganic Ions (page 87)
1. (a) A cation ion is a positively charged ion.
   (b) An anion is a negatively charged ion.
2. (a) Calcium is the a component of teeth and bone. It is involved in muscle contraction, activation of enzymes, blood clotting, and cell signalling.
   (b) Inadequate calcium results in weak bones and teeth, impaired blood clotting, and muscular weakness.
3. (a) NO_3^- is the source of nitrogen for plants and is important in the formation of amino acids and nucleotides.
   (b) Animals get their nitrogen from proteins made in plants or in other animals.
4. (a) HCO_3^-, Cl^-, OH^-, NH_4^+, H^+
   (b) They can accept or donate protons (or electron pairs).

65. Chapter Review (page 88)
No model answer. Summary is the student's own.

66. KEY TERMS: Did You Get it? (page 90)
1. Activation energy (P), amino acids (D), base pairing rule (M), carbohydrates (C), condensation (K), denaturation (I), DNA (Q), enzyme (A), fibrous proteins (G), globular proteins (O), hydrolysis (E), inhibition (B), inorganic ion (N), lipids (J), monomers (F), polymer (H), RNA (L)
2. (a) and (b)

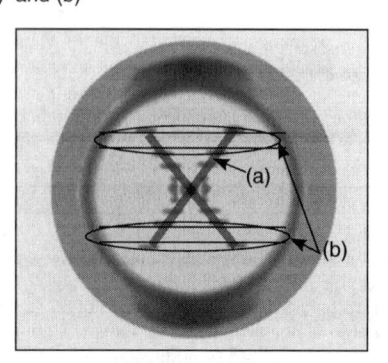

(c) That the helix is continuous, of constant dimensions, and that the phosphate-sugar backbone is on the outside of

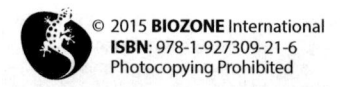

AQA BIOLOGY 1 MODEL ANSWERS

the molecule.
3 (a) Competitive
  (b)

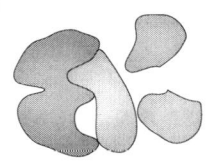

---

67. The Cell is the Unit of Life (page 93)
1. Characteristic features of prokaryotic cells include lack of a membrane-bound nucleus or membrane-bound organelles, typically small cells (0.5-10 µm) with relatively simple organisational structure and a circular chromosome.
2. Characteristic features of eukaryotic cells include the presence of a membrane-bound nucleus and membrane-bound organelles. Large cells with complex cell organisation. DNA is arranged in linear chromosomes.
3. Viruses are classed as non-living because they have no metabolic machinery of their own. The virus can only metabolise and reproduce by utilising the cellular machinery of a cell it has infected.

---

68. Cell Sizes (page 94)
1. (a) *Daphnia*:   1800 µm   1.8 mm
   (b) *Giardia*:   15 µm   0.015 mm
   (c) Nucleus   10 µm   0.01 mm
   (d) *Elodea*:   47 µm   0.047 mm
   (e) Chloroplast   7 µm   0.007 mm
   (f) Paramecium: 250 µm   0.25 mm

2. (a) Chloroplast < nucleus < *Giardia* < *Elodea* < Paramecium < *Daphnia*
   (b) Visible to naked eye: *Daphnia*

3. (a) 0.00025 mm
   (b) 0.45 mm
   (c) 0.0002 mm

---

69. Bacterial Cells (page 95)
1. (a) The nuclear material (DNA) is not contained within a defined nucleus with a nuclear membrane.
   (b) Membrane-bound cellular organelles (e.g. mitochondria, endoplasmic reticulum) are missing.
   (c) Single, circular chromosome sometimes with accessory chromosomes called plasmids.

2. (a) Locomotion - flagella enable bacterial movement.
   (b) Fimbriae are shorter, straighter, and thinner than flagella. They are used for attachment, not locomotion.

3. The bacterial cell wall lies outside the plasma membrane. It is a semi-rigid structure composed of peptidoglycan, and varying amounts of lipopolysaccharides and lipoproteins.

---

70. Plant Cells (page 96)
1. The cell wall provides rigidity, shape, and support for the cell and (through cell turgor) the plant tissues. It also limits the volume of the cell.

2. (a) The vacuole.
   (b) Roles include storage, waste disposal, and growth.

3. (a) Ribosomes in the cytoplasm are 80S ribosomes. Ribosomes in mitochondria and chloroplasts are 70S.
   (b) They have different origins from the cell. 70S ribosomes are also found in bacteria suggesting these organelles have a bacterial origin.

4. Chloroplasts, cell wall

---

71. Identifying Structures in a Plant Cell (page 97)
1. (a) Cytoplasm   (g) Nucleus
   (b) Vacuole   (h) Chromosome
   (c) Starch granule   (i) Nuclear membrane
   (d) Chloroplast   (j) Endoplasmic reticulum
   (e) Mitochondrion   (k) Plasma membrane
   (f) Cell wall

2. 9 cells (1 complete cell, plus the edges of 8 others).

3. Plant cell; it has chloroplasts and a cell wall. It also has a highly geometric cell shape.

4. (a) The cytoplasm is located between the plasma membrane and the nuclear membrane (the material outside the nucleus).
   (b) The cytoplasm comprises a 'watery soup' of dissolved substances. In eukaryotic cells, organelles are found in the cytoplasm.

5. (a) Starch granules, which occur within specialised plastids called leucoplasts. Starch granules are inert inclusions, deposited as a reserve energy store.
   (b) Vacuoles, which are fluid filled cavities bounded by a single membrane. Plant vacuoles contain cell sap, which is an aqueous solution of dissolved food material, ions, waste products, and pigments.

---

72. Animal Cells (page 98)
1. A: Nucleus   B: Plasma membrane   C: Nucleus
2. (a)

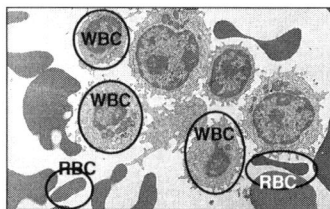

White blood cells (WBC) & red blood cells (RBC)

   (b) Any of: RBCs have no nucleus and they are smaller than the white blood cells. White blood cells have extensions of the plasma membrane (associated with being phagocytic), are larger than the RBCs, and have a nucleus.

3. – Centrioles (absent from higher plants). They are microtubular structures responsible for forming the poles and the spindles during cell division.
   – Desmosomes. These are points of contact between the plasma membranes of neighbouring cells, which allow cells to combine together to form tissues.

---

73. Identifying Structures in an Animal Cell (page 99)
1. (a) Plasma membrane   (e) Lysosome
   (b) Golgi apparatus   (f) Nucleus
   (c) Centriole (TS)   (g) Rough ER
   (d) Mitochondrion   (h) Cytoplasm

2. Centrioles.

3. Plant cells are enclosed by a rigid cellulose cell wall and do not have the capacity for motility or phagocytosis in the way that animal cells do.

4. (a) High protein production and secretion indicated by a relatively large amount of ER and an extensive Golgi apparatus.
   (b) Large number of mitochondria indicate that it is metabolically very active (high respiration rate).

5. It has a membrane-bound nucleus and membrane-bound organelles.

---

74. Cell Structures and Organelles (page 100)
(b) **Name**: Ribosome
Location: In cytoplasm.
Function: Protein synthesis (reading mRNA and add amino acids to polypeptide chain.
Visible in light microscope: No

(c) **Name**: Smooth and rough endoplasmic reticulum
Location: Penetrates the whole cytoplasm
SER function: Site of lipid and carbohydrate metabolism.
RER function: Synthesis of proteins for secretion.
Visible with light microscope: Yes

(d) **Name**: Vacuole
Location: Various locations around the cell but often near the centre, especially in plant cells.
Function: Isolating materials, containing water, providing support, maintaining internal cell pressure, maintaining pH.
Visible with light microscope: yes

(e) **Name**: Golgi apparatus
Location: In cytoplasm associated with the smooth endoplasmic reticulum, often close to the nucleus.
Function: Final modification of proteins and lipids. Sorting and storage for use in the cell or packaging molecules for export.
Visible with light microscope: Yes

(f) **Name**: Cellulose cell wall
Location: Surrounds the cell and lies outside the plasma membrane.
Function: Provides rigidity and strength, and supports the cell against changes in turgor.
Visible with light microscope: Yes

(g) **Name**: Nucleus
Location: Discrete organelle, position is variable.
Function: The control centre of the cell; the site of the nuclear material (DNA).
Visible with light microscope: Yes

(h) **Name**: Chloroplast
Location: Within the cytoplasm
Function: The site of photosynthesis
Visible with light microscope: Yes

(i) **Name**: Mitochondrion
Location: In cytoplasm.
Function: Site of cellular respiration (ATP formation)
Visible with light microscope: Yes

75. Cell Fractionation (page 102)

1. Cell organelles have different densities and spin down at different rates. Smaller organelles take longer to spin down and require a higher centrifugation speed to separate out.

2. The sample is homogenised (broken up) before centrifugation to rupture the cell surface membrane, break open the cell, and release the cell contents.

3. (a) Isotonic solution is needed so that there are no volume changes in the organelles.
   (b) Cool solution prevent self digestion of the organelles by enzymes released during homogenisation.
   (c) Buffered solution prevents pH changes that might denature enzymes and other proteins.

4. (a) Ribosomes and endoplasmic reticulum
   (b) Lysosomes and mitochondria
   (c) Nuclei

76. Identifying Organelles (page 103)

1. (a) Chloroplast
   (b) Plant cells, particularly in leaf and green stems.
   (c) Function: Site of photosynthesis. Captures solar energy to make glucose from CO_2 and water.

2. (a) Golgi apparatus
   (b) Eukaryotic cells (e.g. plant and animal cells)
   (c) Function: Packages substances to be secreted by the cell. Forms a membrane vesicle containing the chemicals for export from the cell (e.g. nerve cells export neurotransmitters, endocrine glands export hormones, digestive gland cells export enzymes).

3. (a) Mitochondrion
   (b) Eukaryotic cells (e.g. plant and animal cells)
   (c) Function: Site of cellular respiration, which releases energy from food (glucose) to fuel metabolism.

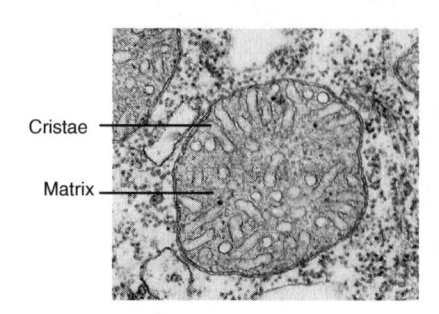

(d) *[Mitochondrion image with Cristae and Matrix labelled]*

4. (a) Endoplasmic reticulum
   (b) Eukaryotic cells (e.g. plant and animal cells)
   (c) Function: Site of protein and membrane synthesis.
   (d) Ribosomes

5. (a) Nucleus
   (b) Eukaryotic cells (e.g. plant and animal cells)
   (c) Function: Controls cell metabolism and functioning of the whole organism. These instructions are inherited from one generation to the next.

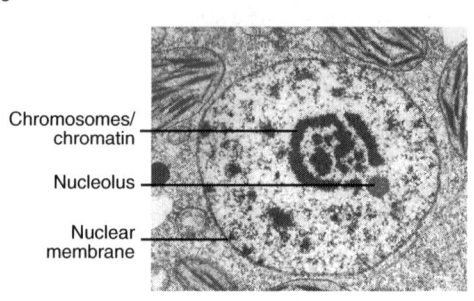

(d) *[Nucleus image with Chromosomes/chromatin, Nucleolus, Nuclear membrane labelled]*

77. Specialisation in Plant Cells (page 104)

1. (b) **Pollen grain**:
   Features: Small, lightweight, often with spikes.
   Role: houses male gamete for sexual reproduction.

   (c) **Palisade parenchyma cell**:
   Features: Column-shaped cell with chloroplasts.
   Role: Primary photosynthetic cells of the leaf.

   (d) **Epidermal cell**:
   Features: Waxy surface on a flat-shaped cell.
   Role: Provides a barrier to water loss on leaf.

   (e) **Vessel element**:
   Features: Rigid remains of a dead cell. No cytoplasm. End walls perforated. Walls are strengthened with lignin fibres.
   Role: Rapid conduction of water through the stem. Provides support for stem/trunk.

   (f) **Stone cell**:
   Features: Very thick lignified cell wall inside the primary cell wall. The cytoplasm is restricted to a small central region of the cell.
   Role: Protection of the seed inside the fruit.

   (g) **Sieve tube member**:
   Features: Long, tube-shaped cell without a nucleus. Cytoplasm continuous with other sieve cells above and below it. Cytoplasmic streaming is evident.
   Role: Responsible for translocation of sugars etc.

   (h) **Root hair cell**:
   Features: Thin cuticle with no waxy layer. High surface area relative to volume.
   Role: Facilitates the uptake of water and ions.

78. Specialisation in Human Cells (page 105)

1. (a) **Phagocytic white blood cell**:
   Features: Phagocytic and highly mobile.
   Role: Destroys pathogens and cellular debris.

   (b) **Erythrocyte**:
   Features: Biconcave cell, lacking mitochondria, nucleus, and most internal membranes. Contains the oxygen-transporting pigment, haemoglobin.
   Role: Uptake, transport, and release of oxygen to the tissues. Some transport of CO_2.

(c) **Squamous epithelial cell**:
   Features: Thin flat cells that line body surfaces.
   Role: Line body surfaces (including internal spaces), providing a membrane in contact with the extracellular environment on one side and anchored to the body cells on the other.
(d) **Skeletal muscle cell**:
   Features: Cylindrical shape with banded myofibrils. Capable of contraction (shortening).
   Role: Move voluntary muscles acting on skeleton. t.
(e) **Ciliated epitheial cell**:
   Features: Simple cells often with a column shaped appearance. Upper surface of cell contains many cilia.
   Role: Cilia sweep back and forth to move particles or fluid. In the bronchioles of the lungs, cilia sweep dust particles up towards the throat.
(f) **Motor neurone**:
   Features: Cell body with a long extension (the axon) ending in synaptic bodies. Axon is insulated with a sheath of fatty material (myelin).
   Role: Rapid conduction of motor nerve impulses from the spinal cord to effectors (e.g. muscle).
(g) **Sperm cell**:
   Features: Motile, flagellated cell with mitochondria. Nucleus forms a large proportion of the cell.
   Role: Male gamete for sexual reproduction. Mitochondria provide the energy for motility.
(h) **Osteocyte**:
   Features: Cell with calcium matrix around it. Fingerlike extensions enable the cell to be supplied with nutrients and wastes to be removed.
   Role: In early stages, secretes the matrix that will be the structural component of bone. Provides strength.

79. Levels of Organisation (page 106)
1. (a) The cellular level.
   (b) The organism.
   (c) The chemical level (DNA).

80. Animal Tissues (page 107)
1. The organisation of cells into specialised tissues allows the tissues to perform particular functions. This improves efficiency of function because different tasks can be shared amongst specialised cells. Energy is saved in not maintaining non-essential organelles in cells that do not require them.
2. (a) **Epithelial tissue**: Lining/protection. Lines internal and external body surfaces and protects the structures underneath.
   (b) **Nervous tissue**: Transmits information (via nerve impulses).
   (c) **Muscle tissue**: Creates movement through contraction.
   (d) **Connective tissues**: Binding, support, and protection.
3. (a) Muscle tissue is made up of long muscle fibre cells made up of myofibrils. The myofibrils are made up of contractile proteins actin and myosin, which cause the muscle fibres to contact when stimulated. The contraction results in movement of the organism itself (locomotion) or movement of an internal organ.
   (b) Nervous tissue is made up of neurones which transmit nerve impulses and glial cells which provide support to the neurones. Neurones have several protrusions (dendrites or axons) from their cell body which allow conduction of nerves impulses to target cells.

81. Plant Tissues (page 108)
1. The three plant tissue systems are dermal, vascular, and ground tissue systems.
2. **Collenchyma**
   Cell type(s): collenchyma cells
   Role: provides flexible support.

   Sclerenchyma
   Cell type(s): sclerenchyma cells
   Role: provides rigid, hard support.

   Root Endodermis
   Cell type(s): endodermal cells
   Role: Selective barrier regulating the passage of substances from the soil to the vascular tissue.

   Pericycle
   Cell type(s): parenchyma cells
   Role: Production of branch roots, synthesis and transport of alkaloids.

   Leaf mesophyll
   Cell type(s): spongy mesophyll, palisade mesophyll
   Role: Main site of photosynthesis in the plant.

   Xylem
   Cell type(s): tracheids, vessels, fibres, parenchyma cells
   Role: Conducts water and dissolved minerals in vascular plants.

   Phloem
   Cell type(s): sieve-tube members, companion cells, parenchyma, fibres, sclereids
   Role: transport of dissolved organic material (including sugars) within vascular plants.

   Epidermis
   Cell type(s): epidermal cells, guard cells, subsidiary cells, and epidermal hairs (trichomes).
   Role: Protection against water loss, regulation of gas exchange, secretion, water and mineral absorption.

82. Viruses (page 109)
1. Viruses are acellular, they have no metabolism by themselves and therefore require living cells in order to replicate.
2. In general a virus is composed of a protein coat surrounding nuclear material (DNA or RNA). All have some means of recognising and interacting with a host cell in order to infect it (e.g. tail fibres or glycoprotein spikes).
3. (a) Glycoprotein spikes enable the virus attach to a host cell.
   (b) Tail fibres enable the phage to attach to a host cell.
   (c) The protein capsid encloses the genetic material and prevent it from immediate degradation inside the host.

83. Optical Microscopes (page 110)
1. (a) Eyepiece lens   (h) In-built light source
   (b) Arm   (i) Eyepiece lens
   (c) Coarse focus knob   (j) Eyepiece focus
   (d) Fine focus knob   (k) Focus knob
   (e) Objective lens   (l) Objective lens
   (f) Mechanical stage   (m) Stage
   (g) Condenser
2. (a) 600X magnification   (b) 600X magnification
3. A compound light microscope produces a flat (2-dimensional) image, which looks through a thin, transparent sample. Dissecting microscopes produce a 3-dimensional image, which looks at the surface details.
4. (a) Dissecting   (b) Compound microscope
5. (a) Magnification is the number of times larger an object appears compared to the actual size.
   (b) Resolution is the ability to distinguish between two objects. The higher the resolution, the higher the magnification can be (and image will still be clear).
6. Steps for setting up a microscope
   1. Turn on the light source.
   2. Rotate the objective lenses until the shortest lens is in place (pointing down towards the stage). This is the lowest power objective lens.
   3. Adjust the distance between the eyepieces so that they are comfortable for your eyes.
   4. Place the slide on the microscope stage. Secure with the sample clips.
   5. Focus and centre the specimen using the low objective lens. Focus firstly with the coarse focus knob, then with the fine focus knob.
   6. Focus the eyepieces to adjust your view.
   7. Adjust the illumination to an appropriate level by adjusting the iris diaphragm and the condenser. The light should

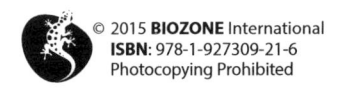

appear on the slide directly below the objective lens, and give an even amount of illumination.
8. Fine tune the illumination so you can view maximum detail on your sample.
9. Focus and centre the specimen using the medium objective lens. Focus firstly with the coarse focus knob, then with the fine focus knob (if needed).
10. Focus and centre the specimen using the high objective lens. Adjust focus using the fine focus knob only.

84. Preparing a Slide (page 112)
1. Thin sections allow light to pass through so features can be more easily seen. Thin sections also reduce the layers of cells (making it easier to see details).
2. The coverslip helps to smooth out the specimen and exclude air bubbles that may obscured features.
3. The onion epidermal cells do not take part in photosynthesis, so they do not contain chloroplasts.
4. Low magnification allows a larger area of the slide to be viewed, allowing specific areas to be located more easily. It also makes focussing easier and protects the slide and lens from damage caused by large movements during coarse focussing.

85. Staining a Slide (page 113)
1. Stains are mostly used to enhance specific features of a sample (e.g. specific organelles).
2. Viable stains are harmless and can be used on living samples. Non-viable staining is used on cell or tissue preparations which are dead.
3. (a) Trypan blue   (c) Aniline sulfate
   (b) Iodine solution   (d) Methylene blue

86. Measuring and Counting Using a Microscope (page 114)
1. 1.4×10^{-2} mm or 14 microns
2. (a) Area: 0.4 mm^2 Volume: 4×10^{-3} mm^3

(b)
	Day 1	Day 2	Day 3
No. of cells counted	4	9	17
Cells in 5 cm^3	5.0×10^6	1.1×10^7	2.1×10^7

3. Volume of central area: $1 \times 1 \times 0.1 = 0.1$ mm^3 = 0.0001 cm^3.
$3 \div 0.0001 = 30\,000$. $30\,000 \times 6 = 180\,000$.
$180\,000 \div 8 = 22\,500 = 2.25 \times 10^4$ pollen grains per anther.

87. Calculating Linear Magnification (page 115)
1. Actual size = image size ÷ magnification
   = 52 000 µm ÷ 140
   = 400 µm (0.4 mm)
2. (a) Actual length of scale line = 10 mm
   Given length of scale line = 0.5 mm
   10 ÷ 0.5 = 20 x magnification
   (b) Measured length = 42 mm
   Magnification = 20 x
   Actual length = 42 ÷ 20 = 2.1 mm
3. 43 mm = 43 000 µm
   Magnification = size of the image ÷ actual size of object
   = 43 000 µm ÷ 2 µm
   = 21 500 x magnification.

88. Electron Microscopes (page 116)
1. The limit of resolution is related to wavelength (about 0.45X the wavelength). The shortest visible light has a wavelength of about 450 nm giving a resolution of 0.45 x 450 nm; close to 200 nm. Points less than 200 nm apart will be perceived as one point or a blur. Electron beams have a shorter wavelength than light so the resolution is much greater (points 0.5 nm apart can be distinguished as separate points; a resolving power that is 400X that of a light microscope).

2. (a) **SEM**: A scanning EM will show the surface features of cells in great detail, which is useful for identification because pollen species have unique surface features. A LM would not provide sufficient detail and TEMs are used for sections, not surface details.
   (b) **TEM**: The very thin sections and high resolution achievable with a transmission EM can reveal the fine ultrastructure of an organelle. A LM would not provide enough magnification nor resolution.
   (c) **Compound light microscope**: A blood cell count requires sufficient magnification to distinguish cell types while retaining an ability to see a large number of cells at once.
   (d) **Dissecting microscope**: A dissecting microscope is the only choice for examining a living organism of this size (1 mm) that must be kept restrained in water while being observed. It increases the magnification enough to view the animal's organs through the transparent carapace.

3. A TEM   E SEM
   B Compound LM   F Compound LM
   C TEM   G Dissecting LM
   D Compound LM   H SEM

89. Cell Division (page 118)
1. (a) Mitosis occurs in body cells (somatic cells) in animals.
   (b) Mitosis is responsible for growth of an organism, repair and replacement of damaged cells, and for asexual reproduction in some eukaryotes.
2. (a) Meiosis occurs in sex organs (testes and ovaries) in animals.
   (b) It produces sex cells (gametes) for the purposes of sexual reproduction.
3. Gametes are haploid (N) because meiosis halves the chromosome number of a somatic cell. Fusion of gametes in fertilisation restores the diploid number for the organism (2N).

90. Mitosis and the Cell Cycle (page 119)
1. The DNA must replicate (during S phase).
2. (a) Interphase: The stage between cell divisions (mitoses). Just before mitosis, the DNA is replicated to form an extra copy of each chromosome (still part of the same chromosome as an extra chromatid).
   (b) Mitosis: In prophase, chromosomes condense, becoming visible as double chromatids. Centrioles move to opposite ends of the cell. In metaphase, spindle fibres form between the centrioles and chromosomes attach to the spindle at the cell equator. In anaphase, chromatids from each chromosome are pulled apart (i.e. homologous chromatids separate). In telophase, chromosomes unwind and two new nuclei form, each new nucleus containing a set of chromosomes. The cell plate forms across the midline where the new cell wall will form.
   (c) Cytokinesis: The cytoplasm divides in two, forming two new cells.
3. Cytokinesis in animal cells involves the formation of a contractile ring of microtubules that constrict to cleave the cell. In plant cell cytokinesis, vesicles deliver cell wall a material to the middle of the cell where a cell plate (a precursor to the new cell wall) forms. The vesicles coalesce to form the plasma membranes of the new cell surfaces.

AQA BIOLOGY 1 MODEL ANSWERS

91. Recognising Stages in Mitosis (page 121)
1. (a) Anaphase (c) Metaphase
   (b) Prophase (d) Telophase
2. (a) Estimate below. This calculation is based on seeing enough of the cell's nucleus. Cells in cytokinesis were included in interphase (not in mitosis).

Stage	No. of cells	% of total cells	Estimated time in stage
Interphase	47	41.5	9 h 57min
Mitosis	66	58.6	14 h 03min
Total	113	100	24 hours

   (b) 66/113 = 0.58
3. The mitotic index will decrease.

92. Regulation of the Cell Cycle (page 122)
1. Cell cycle check points ensure that the cell has the required resources and has met the required conditions to successfully complete the next phase of the cell cycle.
2. (a) The metaphase checkpoint ensures all the chromatids are attached to the spindle and under the proper tension.
   (b) It ensures all daughter cells end up with the correct chromosome complement. Only when all the chromatids are properly attached can the cell proceed to anaphase, in which the chromatids are pulled apart.
3. If the cell cycle was not regulated cells would go into uncontrolled cell division, resulting in the formation of tumours. Cycle regulation also ensures that the cell reaches the appropriate size and volume to divide successfully.

93. Cancer: Cells Out of Control (page 123)
1. (a) Cancerous cells have lost control of the genetic mechanisms regulating the cell cycle so that the cells become immortal. They also lose their specialised functions and are unable to perform their roles.
   (b) There is no resting phase in cell division, the cell begins growth and division as soon as it is formed.
2. (a) Chemotherapy drugs target rapidly growing cells but affecting they rate of cell division.
   (b) Healthy cells, such as those in the hair follicles, are also affected because they also divide rapidly.

94. Binary Fission (page 124)
1. Binary fission is a form of asexual reproduction resulting in the division of a cell into two identical cells.
2. The cross wall is an ingrowth of the cell wall and cell membrane of a cell dividing by binary fission. When its growth is completed, the cross wall completely divides the cell, resulting in the formation of two cells.
3. The generation time is the time taken for a population of bacterial cells to double.
4. Completed table below:

Min	No.	Min	No.	Min	No.
0	1	140	128	260	8192
20	2	160	256	280	16,384
40	4	180	512	300	32,768
60	8	200	1024	320	65,536
80	16	220	2048	340	131,072
100	32	240	4096	360	262,144
120	64				

5. (a) 8   (b) 512   (c) 262 144

95. Replication in Viruses (page 125)
1. (a) Viral DNA replicated in the host cell's nucleus. Viral proteins synthesised in the host cell's cytoplasm.
   (b) Endocytosis is the means by which foreign material is normally engulfed by cells, prior to being destroyed or assimilated. This response of the cell enables the virus to gain entry into the cell.
2. Enveloped viruses use budding to leave the host cell while non-enveloped viruses use apoptosis of the host cell. Enveloped viruses bud by adhering to and becoming engulfed by the cell's plasma membrane, which contributes to the viral envelope. Non-enveloped viruses don't need an envelope so their strategy is to trigger a programmed death of the cell (apoptosis) attracting "clean-up" macrophages, which then become infected by the released viruses.

96. The Role of Membranes in Cells (page 126)
1. (a) Compartments within cells allow enzymatic reactions in the cell to be localised. This achieves greater efficiency in cell function and keeps potentially harmful reactions and substances (e.g. hydrogen peroxide) contained.
   (b) Greater membrane surface area provides a greater area over which membrane-bound reactions can occur. This increases the speed and efficiency with which metabolic reactions can take place.
2. (a) Golgi, mitochondria, chloroplasts, nucleus.
   (b) Mitochondrion - aerobic respiration.
   Golgi - Modifies, sorts, and stores proteins and lipids. Packages molecules for export.
   Chloroplasts - Photosynthesis
   Nucleus - Storage of DNA
   (c) In general, membranes compartmentalise the location of reactions, control the entry and exit of substances and/or provides an enzyme attachment surface.

97. The Structure of Membranes (page 127)
1. (a) Channel and carrier proteins
   (b) Carrier proteins
   (c) Glycoproteins, glycolipids
   (d) Cholesterol
2. Phospholipids have hydrophilic heads and hydrophobic tails. The molecules orientate so that the hydrophilic head is towards the exterior of the membrane and the hydrophobic tail is towards the interior. This forms the a lipid bilayer and the basis of the plasma membrane.
3. (a) Membranes are composed of a phospholipid bilayer in which are embedded proteins, glycoproteins, and glycolipids. The structure is relatively fluid and the proteins are able to move within this fluid matrix.
   (b) This model accounts for the properties we observe in cellular membranes: its fluidity (how its shape is not static and how its components move within the membrane, relative to one-another) and its mosaic nature (the way in which the relative proportions of the membrane components, i.e. proteins, glycoproteins, glycolipids etc, can vary from membrane to membrane). The fluid mosaic model also accounts for how membranes can allow for the selective passage of materials (e.g. through protein channels) and how they enable cell-cell recognition (a result of membrane components such as glycoproteins).
4. (a) Enable the passage of specific molecules into the cell by facilitated diffusion or active transport.
   (b) Provide a hydrophilic pore through the membrane so that water soluble molecules pass easily through.
5. (a) Non-polar molecules can dissolve in the lipid bilayer structure of the membrane and diffuse into the cell whereas the polar molecules must be actively transported through the membrane
   (b) Diffusion of lipid-soluble molecules across the plasma membrane is rapid (increasing efficiency of substrate delivery) and saves energy (transport is passive).
6. Cholesterol lies between the phospholipids and maintains membrane integrity and fluidity (preventing crystallisation).

7. (a)-(c) in any order: oxygen, food (glucose), minerals and trace elements, water.

8. (a) Carbon dioxide   (b) Nitrogenous wastes

9. Plasma membrane:

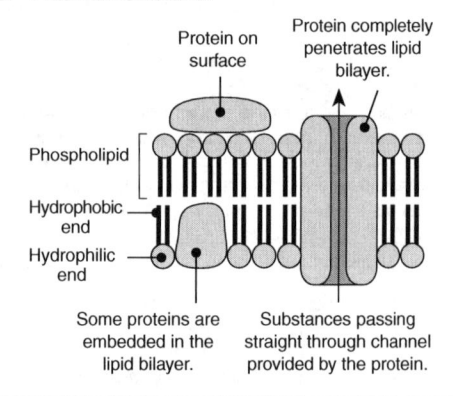

98. How Do We Know? Membrane Structure (page 129)
1. The impressions left in one side of the membrane after freeze fracture give evidence of proteins located within the membrane. Fracturing the membrane allowed scientists to observe the presence of integral membrane proteins which span the membrane lipid bilayer. This supported the fluid mosaic model, in which membrane-bound proteins are able to move relatively freely within the membrane.

2. If the bilayer had a continuous protein coat, the freeze fracture specimen would look flat and uniform when viewed under the electron microscope. The proteins are discrete complexes randomly spaced throughout the lipid bilayer. The bumps observed indicates where the proteins were located.

99. Factors Altering Membrane Permeability (page 130)
1. Washing the beetroot in distilled water removes any pigment that might be present due to leaching as a result of cutting.

2. (a)

Temperature °C	Mean
0	0.0037
20	0.223
40	0.108
60	0.538
90	3

(b) As temperature increases, membrane permeability also increases.
(c) It occurs because there is increasing damage to the tonoplast as temperature is increased.

3. The 0% ethanol solution acts as a control for comparison to the other concentrations.

4. (a) The parafilm stops the ethanol from evaporating.
   (b) The evaporated ethanol when cause a change in concentration of the ethanol/water solution. The results would not be accurate.

5. (a)

Ethanol concentration/ %	Mean
0	0.030
6.25	0.016
12.5	0.023
25	0.082
50	0.925
100	1.184

(b) Absorbance of beetroot samples at varying ethanol concentrations.

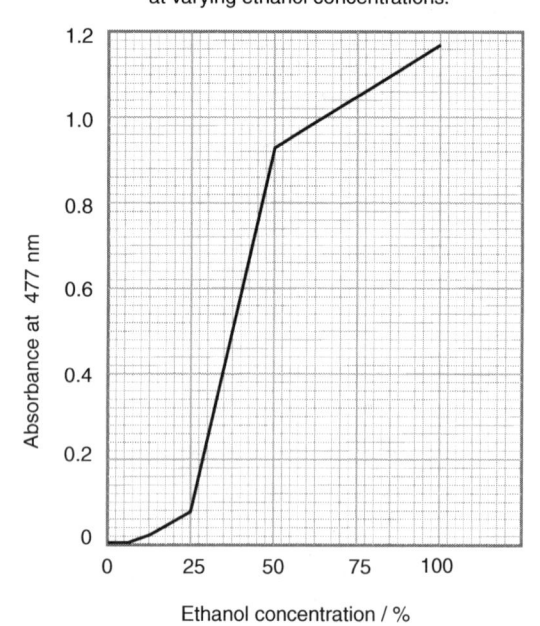

(c) As ethanol concentration increases, membrane permeability also increases.

6. Ethanol causes proteins in the membrane to be denatured. This causes the membrane to lose its selective permeability and become leakier.

100. Diffusion (page 132)
1. Diffusion is the passive movement of particles down a concentration gradient (from high to low concentration).

2. They involve movement of substances across a membrane with no input of energy (they are passive).

3. Facilitated diffusion uses channels to allow ions to pass through the membrane. As ions are charged they can not simply diffuse across the nonpolar interior of the lipid bilayer.

101. Osmosis (page 133)
1. Osmosis is the diffusion of water molecules across a partially permeable membrane from a region of lower solute concentration (higher free water molecule concentration) to a region of higher solute concentration (lower free water molecule concentration).

2. (a) The net movement of water is from right to left:

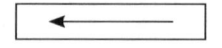

   ←

   (b) The water moved into the dialysis tubing because it contained the sucrose solution, and therefore had a higher solute concentration and a lower concentration of free water molecules. The water moved down its concentration gradient.

3. The height of the water would increase.

102. Water Movement in Plant Cells (page 134)
1. Zero

2. (a) -100 → -200 water moves to cell on the right
   (b) -400 → -500 water moves to cell on the right
   (c) -400 ← -200 water moves to the cell on the left

3. Dissolved solutes lower the water potential (make it more negative).

4. The plasma membrane pushes up against the cell wall which is rigid and stops the cell from bursting.

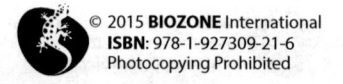

AQA BIOLOGY 1 MODEL ANSWERS

5. (a) Plasmolysis is the pulling away of the plasma membrane from the cell wall, caused by a lack of water in the cell. Turgor is the pressing of the cell membrane against the cell wall as a result of water entering the cell.
   (b) The plant has wilted due to a lack of water. The cells in the plant have plasmolysed and lost their rigidity causing the plant to collapse.

6. (a) Pressure potential generated within plant cells provides the turgor to support unlignified plant tissues.
   (b) Without cell turgor, soft plant tissues (soft stems and flower parts for example) would lose support and wilt. Note that some tissues are supported by structural components such as lignin.

103. Making Dilutions (page 136)

1. (a) 3.75 cm³ stock solution needed
   (b) 2.5 cm³ stock solution needed
   (c) 1.25 cm³ stock solution needed

2. (a) 0.75 mol dm⁻³ = -1838.59 kPa
       0.50 mol dm⁻³ = -1225.73 kPa
       0.25 mol dm⁻³ = -612.86 kPa
       1.00 mol dm⁻³ = -2451.45 kPa
   (b) [Graph: Concentration vs solute potential — linear decreasing plot from 0 at 0.00 mol dm⁻³ to approximately -2500 kPa at 1.00 mol dm⁻³]

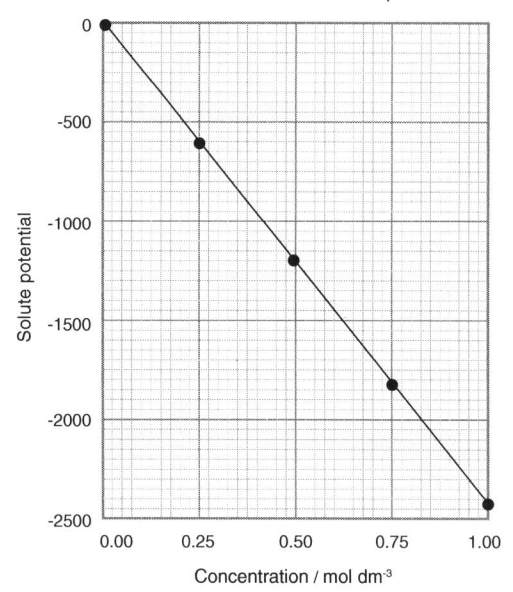

104. Estimating Osmolarity (page 137)

1. Completed table (totals section only)

0.00 Mol dm⁻³		Initial mass (g)	Final mass (g)
Total		15.46	17.22
Change (g)	1.76		
% Change	11.38%		
0.25 Mol dm⁻³		Initial mass (g)	Final mass (g)
Total		19.18	17.93
Change (g)	-1.25		
% Change	-6.52%		
0.50 Mol dm⁻³		Initial mass (g)	Final mass (g)
Total		18.26	16.14
Change (g)	-2.12		
% Change	-11.61%		
0.75 Mol dm⁻³		Initial mass (g)	Final mass (g)
Total		19.16	13.99
Change (g)	-5.17		
% Change	-26.98%		
1.00 Mol dm⁻³		Initial mass (g)	Final mass (g)
Total		16.14	13.00
Change (g)	-3.14		
% Change	-19.45%		

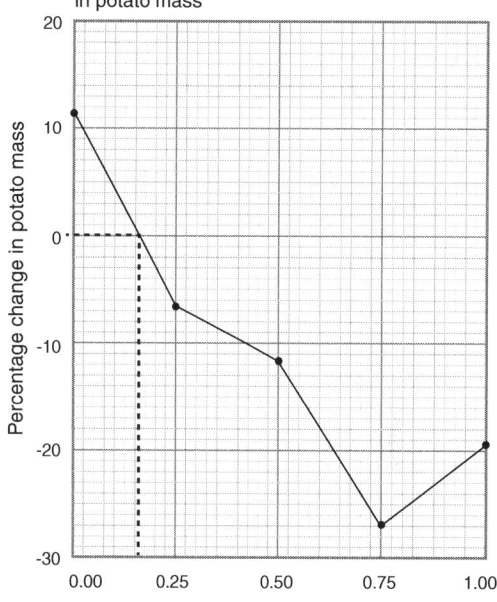

2. [Graph: Sucrose concentration vs percentage change in potato mass — curve decreasing from ~+11% at 0.00 to ~-27% at 0.75, then rising to ~-20% at 1.00; dashed line showing 0% at approximately 0.16 mol dm⁻³]

3. (a) Approximately 0.16 mol dm⁻³
   (b) -365 kPa
   (c) 0 kPa
   (d) -365 kPa

105. Active Transport (page 138)

1. Active transport is the energy using process of moving molecules or ions against their concentration gradient.
2. ATP.
3. Primary active transport uses energy gained directly from ATP. Secondary active transport uses energy in the form of a concentration gradient formed by transport proteins using ATP for energy.

106. Ion Pumps (page 139)

1. ATP (directly or indirectly) supplies the energy to move substances against their concentration gradient.

2. (a) Cotransport describes coupling the movement of a molecule (such as sucrose or glucose) against its concentration gradient to the diffusion of an ion (e.g. H⁺ or Na⁺) down its concentration gradient. Note: An energy requiring ion exchange pump is used to establish this concentration gradient.
   (b) In the gut, a gradient in sodium ions is used to drive the transport of glucose across the epithelium. A Na⁺/K⁺ pump (requiring ATP) establishes an unequal concentration of Na⁺ across the membrane. A specific membrane protein then couples the return of Na⁺ down its concentration gradient to the transport of glucose.
   (c) The glucose diffuses from the epithelial cells of the gut into the blood, where it is transported away. This maintains a low level in the intestinal epithelial cells.

3. Extracellular accumulation of Na⁺ (any two of):
   – maintains the gradient that is used to cotransport useful molecules, such as glucose, into cells.

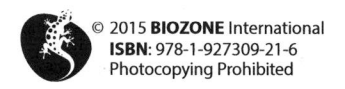

- maintains cell volume by creating an osmotic gradient that drives the absorption of water
- establishes and maintains resting potential in nerve and muscle cells
- provides the driving force for several facilitated membrane transport proteins.

107. Exocytosis and Endocytosis (page 140)
1. Phagocytosis is the engulfment of solid material by endocytosis whereas pinocytosis is the uptake of liquids or fine suspensions by endocytosis.
2. Phagocytosis examples (any of): • Feeding in *Amoeba* by engulfing material using cytoplasmic extensions called pseudopodia. • Ingestion of old red blood cells by Küpffer cells in the liver. • Ingestion of bacteria and cell debris by phagocytic white blood cells.
3. Exocytosis examples: • Secretion of substances from specialised secretory cells in multicellular organisms, e.g. hormones from endocrine cells, digestive secretions from exocrine cells. • Expulsion of wastes from unicellular organisms, e.g. *Paramecium* and *Amoeba* expelling residues from food vacuoles.
4. (a) Oxygen: Diffusion.
   (b) Cellular debris: Phagocytosis.
   (c) Water: Osmosis.
   (d) Glucose: Facilitated diffusion.

108. Cell Recognition (page 141)
1. (a) The MHC is a cluster of tightly linked genes on chromosome 6 in humans. The genes code for MHC antigens (proteins) that are attached to the surfaces of all body cells and are used by the immune system to distinguish its own from foreign tissue.
   (b) This self-recognition system allows the body to immediately identify foreign tissue e.g. a pathogen, and mount an immune attack against it for the protection of the body's own tissues.
2. Any two of the following:
   - after tissue or organs transplants
   - failure to recognise and destroy cancer cells as abnormal
   - during pregnancy when a fetus (foreign tissue) must be carried to term.

109. The Body's Defences (page 142)
1. **Specific resistance** refers to defence against particular (identified) pathogens. It involves a range of specific responses to the pathogen concerned (antibody production and cell-mediated immunity). In contrast, **non-specific resistance** refers to defence against any type of pathogen. it takes the form of physical and chemical barriers against infection, as well as phagocytosis and inflammation

110. Antigenic Variability (page 143)
1. (a) Antigenic variability (constantly occurring changes in viral surface proteins between generations) results in novel antigenic properties to which hosts will not have been exposed and will not have immunity.
   (b) Antigenic shifts represent a combination of two or more different viral strains in a new subtype with new properties and no immunological history in the population. They are therefore potentially more dangerous because the entire population is naive with no immunity. Antigenic drifts are much smaller changes in the virus that occur continually over time. Hosts can generally track these changes through small adjustments in their immune response and these are sufficient to provide resistance.
2. Viruses that are genetically stable do not mutate often and therefore do rapidly change their phenotypes (e.g. surface proteins etc). This means it is simpler to develop a long lasting vaccine as the target for the vaccine is not continually changing.

111. The Action of Phagocytes (page 144)
1. Neutrophils
2. Chemotaxis is the method by which phagocytes locate infections or damaged tissue. By moving up a chemical gradient, phagocytes are able to locate the source of chemical and therefore the source of the infection or damage.
3. By looking at the ratio of white blood cells to red blood cells (which are not involved in the immune response). An elevated white blood cell count indicates infection.
4. Opsonins coat foreign material, marking it as a target for phagocytosis. The opsonins trigger engulfment of the foreign material by phagocytes.

112. The Immune System (page 145)
1. (a) **Humoral immune system**: Production of antibodies against specific antigens. The antibodies disable circulating antigens.
   (b) **Cell-mediated immune system**: Involves the T cells, which destroy pathogens or their toxins by direct contact or by producing substances that regulate the activity of other immune system cells.
2. The presence of an antigen results in the proliferation of specific types of B- and T-cell to target that antigen. Cytokines are also released by macrophages which enhance T-cell activation. More cytokines are released by activated T-cells, and this causes proliferation of other helper T-cells and B-cells.

113. Clonal Selection (page 146)
1. Millions of B-cells form during development. Each B-cell recognises one antigen only, and produces antibodies against it. A pathogen will trigger a response in the B-cell specific that is for it, resulting in proliferation of that B-cell. This is called clonal selection (the antigen selects the B-cell clone that will proliferate).
2. (a) Plasma cells secrete antibodies against antigens (very rapid rate of antibody production).
   (b) The antibodies match the specific antigenic receptors on the B cell. Millions of antibodies are produced and are able to float through the blood and bind corresponding antigens, multiplying the immune response.
3. (a) **Immunological memory**: The result of the differentiation of B cells after the first exposure to an antigen. Those B cells that differentiate into long lived memory cells are present to react quickly and vigorously in the event of a second infection.
   (b) Memory cells respond quickly because they retain an antigenic memory. This means they can rapidly differentiate into antibody-producing plasma cells if they encounter the same antigen again.

114. Antibodies (page 147)
1. Antibodies consist of two heavy (long) peptide chains each attached to a light (short) peptide chain, commonly forming a Y configuration. The variable region at the ends of the heavy and light chains form the antigen binding sites.
2. (a) **Agglutinins** bind antigens together inactivating them and stopping them from infecting or damaging cells.
   (b) **Antitoxins** bind and neutralise toxins, stopping them from damaging cells.
   (c) **Opsonins** act as tags that the antibodies can recognise, enhancing the ability of phagocytes to engulf and destroy antigens.

115. Acquired Immunity (page 148)
1. (a) Immunity as a result of antibodies transferred from one person to another. In this case, the recipient does not make the antibodies themselves.
   (b) **Naturally acquired** passive immunity arises as a result of antibodies passing from the mother to the foetus/infant via the placenta/breast milk. **Artificially acquired** passive immunity arises as a result of injection with immune serums e.g. in antivenoms.

2. (a) Newborns need to be supplied with maternal antibodies because they have not yet had exposure to the everyday microbes in their environment and must be born with operational defence mechanisms.
    (b) The antibody "supply" is (ideally) supplemented with antibodies in breast milk because it takes time for the infant's immune system to become fully functional. During this time, the supply of antibodies received during pregnancy will decline.
    (c) Yes. Breast feeding will provide the infant with a naturally acquired passive immunity to help protect it against infections while its immune system develops. Without this acquisition, the infant is more vulnerable to everyday infections against which you already have immunity but he/she does not.

3. (a) Immunity as a result of the immune response caused by exposure to a microbe or its toxins.
    (b) **Naturally acquired** active immunity arises as a result of exposure to an antigen such as a pathogen, e.g. natural immunity to chickenpox. **Artificially acquired** active immunity arises as a result of vaccination, e.g. any childhood disease for which vaccinations are given: diphtheria, measles, mumps, polio etc.

4. (a) The primary response is of a smaller magnitude than the secondary response. The primary response takes longer to develop and is over more quickly than the secondary response, which is rapid and long lasting.
    (b) The immune system has already been prepared to respond to the antigen by the first exposure to it. When exposed to the same antigen again, it can respond quickly with rapid production of antibodies.

5. (a) Herd immunity refers to the protection that unimmunised people have against a circulating disease by virtue of the fact that most of the population are immunised.
    (b) Once the population contains a high proportion of non-vaccinated people, herd immunity is lost and a circulating disease can spread very rapidly through the community, raising public health costs and contributing to lost productivity.

116. Vaccines and Vaccination (page 150)

1. Attenuated viruses are more effective in the long term because they tend to replicate in the body, and the original dose therefore increases over time. Such vaccines are derived from mutations accumulated over time in a laboratory culture, so there is always a risk that they will back-mutate to a virulent form.

2. High vaccination rates increase the rates of immunity within a population, so fewer people will contract the disease with each outbreak. Transmission of the disease is limited because there are fewer susceptible hosts. Eventually, the disease cannot be supported and no longer occurs.

3. Factors making eradication difficult include (any of):
    - Rapid mutation rates in the pathogen, which make the vaccine ineffective after a short time (e.g. HIV and influenza)
    - Presence of an animal reservoir
    - Movement of populations, so that a proportion of the population avoids vaccination
    - Low frequency or rate of vaccination, which can be influenced by the social or political climate. Unstable political environments make robust vaccination programmes difficult to implement. Widespread poverty or famine can make vaccination a low priority.

4. (a) The influenza virus is constantly undergoing genetic change (mutation) to produce new strains. Therefore it is not possible to produce one influenza vaccination that will protect an individual for life.
    (b) Each years' vaccine is based on the strains present in the previous season, if the predictions are wrong, the flu vaccine will not be effective and the influenza strain may become common in the population.

5. The number of reported cases of whooping cough increased significantly. They only began to drop again when vaccination rates increased again.

117. Questions About Vaccines (page 152)

1. (a) The rate decreases from over 90% to ~80% before beginning to rise again around 2004-2005.
    (b) The drop in vaccination rates coincided with an increase in measles cases 2001-2003, but the pattern is inconsistent after 2005, with cases increasing, falling, and then increasing despite a recovery in vaccination rates.

2. (a) and (b) Answers depend on student's research and opinion. Reasons for opting out of vaccination programmes include religious and personal beliefs.

118. HIV/AIDS (page 153)

1. (a) HIV infects helper T-cell lymphocytes.
    (b) HIV infects and kills the cells of the immune system that normally defend the body from infection. This leaves the body vulnerable to invasion by microbes that would not normally infect a healthy person.

2. The virus rapidly increases in numbers within the first year of infection, followed by a large drop off in numbers in the second year. Over the next 3-10 years, the HIV population gradually increases again.

3. Antibiotics are effective only against living bacterial cells. Viruses have none of the metabolic processes that are targeted by antibiotics so are unaffected by them.

4. (a) HIV enters a T cell by attaching to the CD4 receptors on the cell surface, and fusing with the cell's plasma membrane.
    (b) Reverse transcriptase transcribes the viral RNA into viral DNA. This must occur for the viral genes to be able to integrate into the host's chromosomes where it stays as a provirus.
    (c) The provirus remains integrated with the host chromosome and persists as a latent infection. This means that it can reinfect new host cells whenever the DNA is replicated..

5. (a) Retroviruses integrate their genetic material into the host's own chromosome, so their latency protects them from drugs that target actively replicating viral particles.
    (b) Without revere transcriptase, the viral RNA cannot be transcribed into viral DNA and it can neither integrate into the host's chromosome nor use the host cell's enzymes to transcribe its genes.

119. Monoclonal Antibodies (page 155)

1. (a) A monoclonal antibody is an artificially produced antibody that bonds to and neutralises one specific type of antigen.
    (b) Monoclonal antibodies bind to a specific antigen in the same way as normal antibodies.

2   (a) When bound, the OKT3 antibody deactivates the TCR/CD3 complex making transplanted organs safe from attack by T-cells.
    (b) OKT3 is effective as it only targets the CD3 receptor.

3. (a) The reaction zone contains soluble mouse monoclonal anti-HCG AB-enzyme conjugates which bind to the HCG hormone.
    (b) The test zone contains polyclonal anti-HCG antibodies, which also bind HCG, and a dye. The enzyme catalyses a reaction with the dye causing a colour change.
    (c) In the control zone, unbound antibody-enzyme conjugates bind with the anti-mouse antibodies. The enzyme catalyses a second colour change reaction to confirm the test is working.

4. Only one band would be present (the one showing the test has run correctly).

5. Student's own response. Some points include: Production of monoclonal antibodies requires the use of animal factories (e.g. mice). Potentially, these issues can be solved with *in vitro* techniques. To make monoclonal ABs that are stable in humans may also require that the mice are transgenic for a specific human gene. Despite being engineered for

compatibility, some monoclonal antibodies still cause severe or fatal reactions in humans.

120. Herceptin: A Modern Monoclonal (page 157)
1. (a) HER2+ cells have the same receptors as normal cells, just more of them. The immune system does not recognise this as foreign.
   (b) The attachment of a foreign antibody (Herceptin) to HER2 surface proteins alerts the immune system, which then targets the Herceptin (and the HER2 protein to which it is attached).
   (c) The use of Herceptin increases the chances of survival especially after four years of chemotherapy.

121. Chapter Review (page 158)
No model answer. Summary is the student's own.

122. KEY TERMS: Did You Get It? (page 160)
1. antibody (Q), antigen (J), cell wall (G), chloroplast (D), clonal selection (M), eukaryotic (O), magnification (B), mitochondrion (K), nucleus (I), optical microscope (P), organelle (F), pathogen (E), plasma membrane (N), prokaryotic (L), resolution (C), vaccination (H), virus (A)

2. (a) Mitochondrion   (c) Chloroplast
   (b) Plant and animal cell (d) Plant cell

3. Transport of molecules though the plasma membrane can be active or passive. Active transport requires the input of energy whereas passive transport does not. Passive transport involves the movement of molecules from high concentration to low concentration (down a concentration gradient). Simple diffusion can occur directly across the membrane. Facilitated diffusion involves proteins in the plasma membrane which help molecules or ions to move through. Active transport involves membrane proteins which couple the energy provided by ATP to the movement of molecules or ions against their concentration gradient.

123. Limitations to Cell Size (page 163)
1. Cube   Surface area   Volume   Ratio
    3 cm: 3 x 3 x 6 = 54   3 x 3 x 3 = 27   2.0 to 1
    4 cm: 4 x 4 x 6 = 96   4 x 4 x 4 = 64   1.5 to 1
    5 cm: 5 x 5 x 6 = 150   5 x 5 x 5 = 125   1.2 to 1

2. Surface area to volume graph:
   (Graph: Volume / cm^3 vs Surface area / cm^2; points plotted at (24:8), (54:27), (96:64), (150:125))

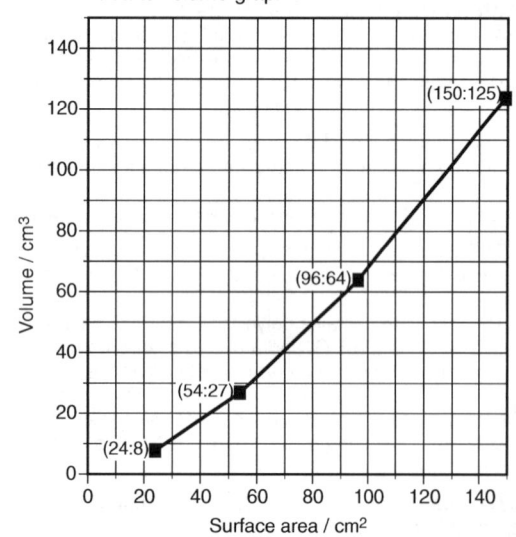

3. Volume

4. Increasing size leads to less surface area for a given volume. The surface area to volume ratio decreases.

5. (a)

Cube	1	2	3
Total volume	1	8	64
Volume not pink	0.125 (0.5^3)	3.375 (1.5^3)	42.8 (3.5^3)
Diffused volume	0.875	4.625	21.2
Percentage diffusion	87.5	57.8	33.1

(b) An increase in cell size reduces the ability of diffusion to transport molecules into and out of a cell at the rate required to maintain the cell's original metabolic rate. (i.e. volume increases faster that surface area and thus the proportion of molecules diffusing across the plasma membrane decreases in relation to the size of the cell).

6. A cell measuring 1 cm x 1 cm x 1 cm has a surface area of 6 cm^2. Eight of them will have a volume of 8 cm^3 but a surface area of 48 cm^2. A cell measuring 2 cm x 2 cm x 2 cm will have a volume of 8 cm^3 but a surface area of only 24 cm^2. Thus eight small cells are more able to acquire nutrients due to their larger surface area to volume ratios.

124. Exchange Surfaces (page 165)
1. Cellular respiration refers to production of ATP via oxidation of glucose. Gas exchange refers to the way in which respiratory gases are exchanged with the environment. Oxygen is required to drive the reactions of cellular respiration. CO_2 is a waste product.

2. (a) Oxygen and CO_2 (b) Diffusion.

3. A gas exchange surface provides a surface across which gases can diffuse.

4. (a) Associated with mechanisms (e.g. blood flow) to maintain the concentration gradient.
   (b) Large surface area to provide for high rates of gas exchange (enough to meet the organism's needs).
   (c) Thin membrane that does not present a large barrier to diffusion of gases.

5. Root hairs increase the surface area for absorption of water and minerals.

6. (a) Rate of diffusion increases
   (b) Rate of diffusion increases
   (c) Rate of diffusion decreases

7. Mammals maintain an oxygen gradient by constantly moving air into and out of the lungs by breathing. Fresh air is breathed in (inspiration), oxygen moves into the blood, and oxygen-deficient air is expelled (expiration).

125. Gas Exchange in Animals (page 167)
1. (a) Provides adequate supply and removal of respiratory gases necessary for an active lifestyle.
   (b) Enables animals to attain a larger size (as they are freed from a dependence on direct diffusion of gases across thin body surfaces).

2. (a) Air breathers produce mucus that keeps the gas exchange surface moist.
   (b) Some water vapour is present in lungs as a result of metabolism.

3. Gills are external structures and need support from a dense medium (water). In air, they would collapse.

4. Breathing in and out keeps air moving and maintains the concentration gradient for the diffusion of gases (carbon dioxide out and oxygen in).

126. Gas Exchange in Insects (page 168)
1. In insect tracheae, gases move by diffusion directly into the tissues. Gases diffuse into and out of the fluid at the end of the tracheole, and the fluid acts as the medium for gas exchange into the tissues.

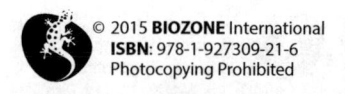

2. Valves present in the spiracles control the rate of entry and exit of air into and out of the tracheal system. This enables the rate of gas exchange to be regulated according to the changing activity levels (and therefore gas exchange requirements) of the insect.
3. Ventilation occurs when the insect makes rhythmic body movements helping to move the air in and out of the tracheae.
4. Tracheal systems provide direct delivery of oxygen to the tissues. This system is rapid and efficient for small sized organisms and reduces reliance on water (water is a necessity for organisms relying on diffusion across a moist body surface). A reduced dependence on freely available water has allowed insects to colonise some of the driest places on Earth.

127. Gas Exchange in Fish (page 169)
1. (a)-(c) any of, in any order:
   - Greatly folded surface of gills (high surface area).
   - Gills supported and kept apart from each other by the gas exchange medium (water).
   - Water flow across the gill surface is opposite to that of the blood flow in the gill capillaries (countercurrent), facilitating oxygen uptake.
   - Pumping mechanism of operculum aids movement of the water across the gas exchange surface.
2. Ventilation (moving water across the gill surface) prevents stagnation of the water at the gill surface and maintains the concentration gradient necessary for continued gas exchange.
3. (a) **Pumping**: Operculum acts as a pump, drawing water past the gill filaments.
   (b) **Continuous swimming**: Continuous (usually rapid) swimming with the mouth open produces a constant flow of water over the gill filaments.
4. In countercurrent flow, oxygen-rich water flows over the gill filaments in the opposite direction to the blood flow through the gill filaments. Blood in the capillaries always encounters water with a higher oxygen concentration so the concentration gradient for diffusion into the blood is maintained across the entire gill.
5. (a) As blood flows through the gill capillaries (gaining oxygen) it encounters blood of increasing oxygen content, so a diffusion gradient is maintained across the entire gill surface.
   (b) In parallel flow, the oxygen concentration in the blood and the water would quickly equalise and diffusion into the blood would stop.
6. Oxygen availability in water is low anyway, so anything that lowers this still further (high temperature of decomposition of organic material) increases the vulnerability of fish to oxygen deprivation. This is especially so for fish with high oxygen requirements such as trout and salmon.

128. Gas Exchange in Plants (page 171)
1. (a) and (b) Any two of:
   - Thin blade to maximise the surface area for light capture and gas exchanges.
   - Loosely packed mesophyll facilitates gas movements into and out of the leaf.
   - Transparent so there is no impairment to light entry.
   - Waterproof cuticle reduces transpirational water losses.
2. (a) Net gas exchange (no photosynthesis): net use of oxygen and net production of carbon dioxide.
   (b) Net gas exchange (photosynthesis): net use of carbon dioxide and net production of oxygen.
3. (a) Facilitate diffusion of gases into and out of the leaf.
   (b) Provide a large surface area for gas exchanges (around the cell.
4. Stomata regulate the entry and exit of gases into and out of the leaf (they also regulate water loss).
5. (a) Stomatal opening: Active transport of potassium ions into the guard cells (which lowers the water potential of the guard cells) is followed by osmotic influx of water. This causes the guard cells to swell and become turgid. The structure of the guard cell walls causes them to buckle out, opening the stoma.
   (b) Stomatal closure: Potassium ions leave the guard cell (making the water potential of the guard cells less negative) and water follows by osmosis. The guard cells become flaccid and sag together closing the stoma.

129. Adaptations of Xerophytes (page 173)
1. A xerophyte is a plant specifically adapted to grow in arid (dry) environments.
2. (a)-(c), three in any order:
   - Modification of leaves to reduce transpirational loss (e.g. spines, curling, leaf hairs).
   - Shallow, but extensive fibrous root system to extend area from which water is taken and to take advantage of overnight condensation.
   - Water storage in stems or leaves.
   - Rounded, squat shape of plant body to reduce surface area for water loss.
3. A moist microenvironment reduces the gradient in water potential between the leaf and the air, so there is less tendency for water to leave the plant.
4. A low surface area to volume ration means that, relative to the plant's volume, there is very little surface area over which water can be lost.

130. The Human Gas Exchange System (page 174)
1. (a) The structural arrangement (lobes, each with its own bronchus and dividing many times before terminating in numerous alveoli) provides an immense surface area for gas exchange.
   (b) Gas exchange takes place in the alveoli.
2. The alveolar-capillary membrane is the layered junction between the alveolar cells, the endothelial cells of the capillaries, and their associated basement membranes. It provides a surface across which gases can move freely by diffusion.
3. Surfactant reduces the surface tension of the lung tissue and counteracts the tendency of the alveoli to recoil inward and stick together after each expiration.
4. Completed table as below:

Region	Cartilage	Ciliated epithelium	Goblet cells (mucus)	Smooth muscle	Connective tissue
❶ Trachea	✓	✓	✓	✓	✓
❷ Bronchus	✓	✓	✓	✓	✓
❸ Bronchioles	gradually lost	✓	✓	✓	✓
❹ Alveolar duct	✗	✗	✗	✓	✓
❺ Alveoli	✗	✗	✗	very little	✓

5. Respiratory distress syndrome: The lack of surfactant and high surface tension in the alveoli result in the collapse of the lungs to an uninflated state after each breath. Breathing is difficult and laboured, oxygen delivery is inadequate and, if untreated, death usually follows in a few hours.

131. Breathing in Humans (page 176)
1. Breathing ventilates the lungs, renewing the supply of fresh (high oxygen) air while expelling air high in CO_2 (gained as a result of gas exchanges in the tissues).
2. Breathing is the result of muscle contraction and relaxation that increases and decreases the volume of the thoracic cavity. The pressure changes that accompany the volume changes cause air to move in and out of the lungs.
3. (a) Quiet breathing: External intercostal muscles and diaphragm contract. Lung volume increases and air flows into the lungs (inspiration). Expiration occurs through

elastic recoil of the ribcage and lung tissue (air flows passively out to equalise with outside air pressure).
(b) In active breathing, muscular contraction is involved in both inspiration and expiration (expiration is not passive).

4. (a) External intercostals and diaphragm.
   (b) Internal intercostals and abdominal muscles

5. (a) Internal intercostals and abdominal muscles
   (b) External intercostals and diaphragm.

6. Antagonistic muscles bring about the changes in thoracic volume that enable air to be moved in and out of the lungs. The muscles for inspiration are in opposition to those for expiration. When one set is contracting, the other is relaxed.

132. Measuring Lung Function (page 177)

1. (a) Taller people generally have larger lung volumes and capacities.
   (b) Males have larger lung volumes and capacities than females.
   (c) After adulthood, lung volume and capacity declines with age. Children have smaller lung volumes and lung capacities than adults.

2. (a) People use only a small proportion of their lung volume in normal breathing (tidal volume) so a forced volume gives a more useful indicator or lung function..
   (b) Spirometry can be used to measure the extent of recovery of lung function after treatment.

3. (a) Tidal volume   vol: 0.5 L
   (b) Expiratory reserve volume   vol: 1.0 L
   (c) Residual volume   vol: 1.2 L
   (d) Inspiratory capacity   vol: 3.8 L
   (e) Vital capacity   vol: 4.8 L
   (f) Total lung capacity   vol: 6.0 L

4. G: Tidal volume is increasing as a result of exercise.

5. PV: 15 x 0.4 = 6 L

6. (a) During strenuous exercise, PV increases markedly.
   (b) Increased PV is achieved as a result of an increase in both breathing rate and tidal volume.

7. (a) There is 90X more CO_2 in exhaled air than in inhaled air (3.6 ÷ 0.04).
   (b) The CO_2 is the product of cellular respiration in the tissues. Note: Some texts give a value of 4.0% for exhaled air (100X the CO_2 content of inhaled air).
   (c) The dead space air is not involved in gas exchange therefore retains a higher oxygen content than the air that leaves the alveoli air. This raises the oxygen content of the expired air.

133. Investigating Ventilation in Humans (page 179)

1. (a) 3.15 dm^3
   (b) 3.75 dm^3
   (c) These results are expected. In general males are physically larger than females and so their lung capacity will also be larger.

2. (a) and (b)

[Graph: Height vs vital capacity, Vital capacity / dm^3 vs Height / cm, showing Male (○) and Female (●) data points with trend lines]

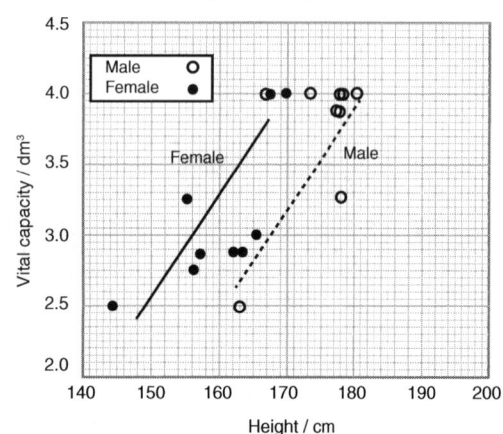

(c) There is a positive correlation between height and vital capacity.

134. Respiratory Diseases (page 180)
Note Activity 132 should also be included as a related activity.

1. Obstructive lung diseases are those in which the air cannot reach the gas exchange region of the lung, as occurs as a result of airway constriction (asthma), excess mucus (bronchitis), or reduced lung elasticity (emphysema). Restrictive lung diseases result from scarring of the gas exchange surface (fibrosis) which results in stiffening and lack of lung expansion. Such diseases result from inhalation of dusts (e.g. coal dust).

2. (a) In a chronic obstructive pulmonary disease, the FEV_1 is reduced disproportionately more than the FVC resulting in an FEV_1/FVC ratio less than 70%.
   (b) Although the FEV_1/FVC ratio is reduced in asthmatics, there will be an improvement in the ratio towards the normal range (80%+) after treatment.
   (c) In a restrictive lung disease, both FEV1 and the FVC are compromised equally. Although measures of lung function indicate impairment, the FEV1/FVC ratio remains high.

3. Restrictive lung diseases, such as **fibrosis**, impair lung function because the gas exchange surface becomes scarred, less flexible, and thicker. This reduces the amount of alveolar expansion possible and reduces the diffusion efficiency across the gas exchange surface.

4. Many restrictive diseases are caused by inhalation of dusts and pollutants associated with particular occupations, e.g. asbestos workers, coal miners, beryllium miners, cement workers etc.

5. In an asthma attack, histamine is released from sensitized mast cells. The histamine causes airway constriction, accumulation of fluid and mucus, and inability to breathe.

135. Risk Factors for Lung Disease (page 182)

1. (a) A long term study is important with a chronic disease that develops slowly because it may take many years for convincing relationships to become evident in the data.
   (b) The study also showed that there was a convincing 20 year lag in the development of lung cancer in smokers.

2. Older age groups were more likely to be exposed to asbestos and over time this group has experienced more cases of asbestosis. In younger age groups there has been little exposure to asbestos (asbestos use declined) and so the incidence rate has diminished over time.

136 Reducing the Risk of Lung Disease (page 183)

1. (a) The increase in federal taxes and warnings about smoking is coincident with a decrease in the number of people smoking in the United States. The strong relationship suggests cause and effect.
   (b) The release of the Surgeon General's report.

2. Evidence shows the simplest way to reduce the risk of dying from lung cancer is to either stop smoking or not start in the first place.

3. (a) 58%   (b) 81%

4. The earlier a person stops smoking, the lower their risk of dying from lung cancer.

137. The Role of the Digestive System (page 184)

1. (a) Food is broken down mechanically (e.g. by chewing) and by chemical means (e.g. digestive enzymes).
   (b) Food must be broken down into smaller molecules so that it can be absorbed across the intestinal wall and utilized by the body.

2. There are several different types of digestive enzymes, each hydrolyses (breaks down) different types of food. Proteases hydrolyse proteins and peptides into amino acids, Amylases

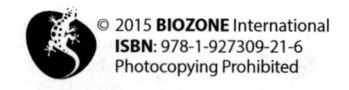

hydrolyse carbohydrates, and lipases hydrolyse lipids.

138. Digestion (page 185)
1. HCl activates pepsinogen into its active form, pepsin. It also helps to kill any bacteria in food and denatures proteins.
2. Bile emulsifies fats, so the presence of acid and fat in the duodenum indicates (1) that fat is present and requiring digestion and (2) the acid must be neutralised by the alkaline bile so that lipases can act on the fat.
3. (a) Duodenum, jejunum, ileum
   (b) Duodenum - most of the chemical digestion occurs here. Jejunum and ileum - most of the absorption occurs here.
4. The brush border refers to the microvilli projecting from each intestinal cell. The brush border increases surface area nad contains the membrane-bound enzymes that complete the digestion of proteins and carbohydrates.
5. (a) Enzymes are found in the pancreatic and intestinal juices, and in bile, which are all secreted into the duodenum. Enzymes are also bound to the surfaces of epithelial cells.
   (b) The secretions must be alkaline to neutralise the acid pH of the chyme entering the duodenum and create the optimal environment for the pancreatic and intestinal enzymes to work.

139. Optimal pH of Digestive Enzymes (page 187)
1. [Graph: pH vs reaction rate α-amylase, rate of reaction / Δ absorbance s^{-1}, peaking near pH 6.5]

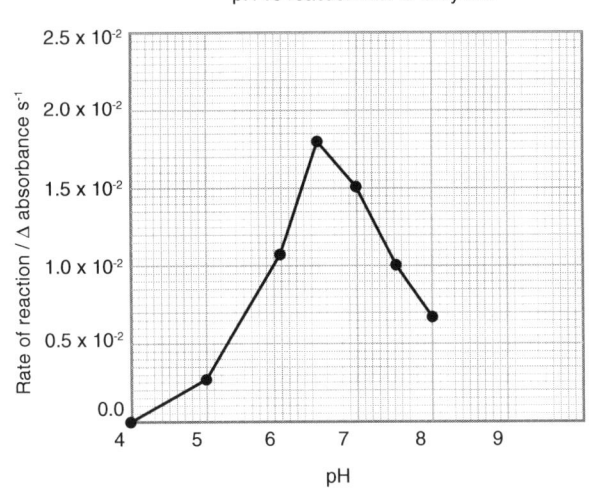

   [Graph: pH vs reaction rate pepsin, rate of reaction / Δ absorbance s^{-1}, peaking near pH 1.7]

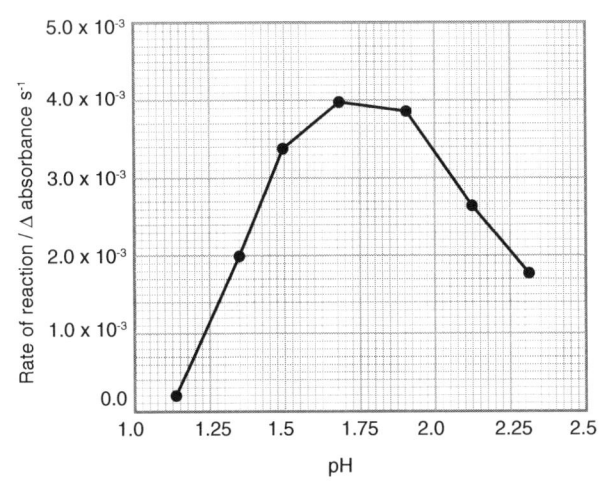

2. (a) 6.5
   (b) α-amylase is found in the saliva of the mouth. As this has a pH close to neutral it would be expected that the optimal pH of α-amylase would also be close to neutral.

   (c) The enzyme was denatured.
3. (a) 1.7
   (b) Pepsin is found in the stomach, which has a pH of about 2. It is therefore expected that the optimal pH of pepsin would close to this.

140. Absorption (page 188)
1. (a) Having no starch in the water sets up a concentration gradient and simulates the intestinal-blood concentration environment in the body.
   (b) Large molecules cannot pass through the partially permeable membranes of cells. They must be broken down into smaller molecules first.
2. Amylase hydrolyses starch into the disaccharide maltose. The maltase enzyme then hydrolyses maltose into glucose. Glucose can then be absorbed across the intestine and utilised by the body.
3. Amylase produced in the salivary glands is denatured in the stomach. More amylase is secreted into the chyme by the pancreas once the food has passed the stomach.
4. (a) Active transport   (c) Active transport
   (b) Facilitated diffusion   (d) Active transport
5. Micelles hold the fatty acids in suspension and transport them to the surface of the intestinal epithelial cells.
6. The nutrients are constantly transported away once they are absorbed into the blood.

141. Transport and Exchange in Animals (page 190)
1. As body mass increases the surface area to volume ratio decreases. As this occurs diffusion becomes too inefficient and slow to provide raw materials quickly enough to all the cells of larger animals. Mass transport systems are required to transport materials to and from where they are needed.
2. (a) In vertebrates mass transport is used to transport materials around the body.
   (b) Mass transport systems allow materials to be moved over a long distance in complex multicellular organisms. In contrast, small organisms such as the flatworm or single celled eukaryotes have a surface area to volume ratio large enough to allow for materials to be efficiently transported by diffusion.
   (c) The tissues and either the gills or lungs.

142. Circulatory Fluids (page 191)
1. (a) and (b), any two in any order: Clotting wounds, internal defence, transport of nutrients.
2. Vertebrate blood transports respiratory gases (oxygen and carbon dioxide) whereas insect haemolymph does not.
3. Maintain body pressure for moulting and antifreeze for over wintering.
4. Red blood cells do not have nuclei. Red blood cells transport oxygen about the body. White blood cells are involved in immune responses.
5. 10% of the haemolymph is cells where as 40-50% of blood is cells.

143. Haemoglobins (page 192)
1. (a) Respiratory pigments can bind reversibly with oxygen. They may bind and carry several oxygen molecules (and therefore increase the amount that can be carried over what can be dissolved in the plasma, which is very low).
   (b) The number of metal-containing prosthetic groups.
2. Organisms with a high metabolic activity (therefore high oxygen demand) have haemoglobins with a greater oxygen carrying capacity (values are highest in endothermic homeotherms, i.e. birds and mammals).
3. Large MW respiratory pigments are too large to be held within cells and must be carried dissolved in the plasma.

144. Gas Transport in Humans (page 193)
1. (a) Oxygen is high in the lung alveoli and in the capillaries leaving the lung.
   (b) Carbon dioxide is high in the capillaries leaving the tissues and in the cells of the body tissues.
2. Haemoglobin binds oxygen reversibly, taking up oxygen when oxygen tensions are high (lungs), carry oxygen to where it is required (the tissues) and release it.
3. (a) As oxygen level in the blood increases, more oxygen combines with haemoglobin. However, the relationship is not linear: Hb saturation remains high even when blood oxygen levels fall very low.
   (b) When oxygen level (partial pressure) in the blood or tissues is low, haemoglobin saturation declines markedly and oxygen is released (to the tissues).
4. (a) Fetal Hb has a higher affinity for oxygen than adult Hb (it can carry 20-30% more oxygen).
   (b) This higher affinity is necessary because it enables oxygen to pass from the maternal Hb to the fetal Hb across the placenta.
5. (a) The Bohr effect.
   (b) Actively respiring tissue consumes a lot of oxygen and generates a lot of carbon dioxide. This lowers tissue pH causing more oxygen to be released from the haemoglobin to where it is required.
6. Myoglobin preferentially picks up oxygen from Hb and is able to act as an oxygen store in the muscle.
7. Any two of: **Haemoglobin**, which picks up H^+ generated by the dissociation of carbonic acid. **Bicarbonate** alone (from this dissociation), and combined with Na^+ (from the dissociation of NaCl). **Blood proteins**.

145. The Mammalian Transport System (page 195)
1. (a) Head   (d) Gut (intestines)
   (b) Lungs   (e) Kidneys
   (c) Liver   (f) Genitals/lower body
2. Circle pulmonary artery and pulmonary vein.

146. Arteries (page 196)
1. (a) Tunica externa   (c) Endothelium
   (b) Tunica media   (d) Blood (or lumen)
2. Thick, elastic walls are required in order to withstand and maintain the high pressure of the blood being pumped from the heart. The elasticity also helps to even out the surges occurring with each heart beat.
3. The smooth muscle around arteries helps to regulate blood flow and pressure. By contracting or relaxing it alters the diameter of the artery and adjusts the volume of blood as required.
4. Arteries have layers of muscle and elastic tissue, which enables them to expand (vasodilation) or constrict (vasoconstriction) to regulate the blood pressure by increasing or decreasing the diameter of the artery lumen.

147. Veins (page 197)
1. (a) Veins have less elastic and muscle tissue than arteries.
   (b) Veins have a larger lumen than arteries.
2. Blood in arteries travels at high pressure, so arteries are thick, strong and stretchy, with a lot of elastic tissue to resist and maintain the pressure. Blood in veins travels at lower pressure so veins do not need to be as strong. They have thinner layers of muscle and elastic tissue and a relatively larger lumen.
3. Valves (with muscular movements) help to return venous blood to the heart by preventing backflow away from the heart.
4. Venous blood oozes out in an even flow from a wound because it has lost a lot of pressure after passing through the narrow capillary vessels (with their high resistance to flow). Arterial blood spurts out rapidly because it is being pumped directly from the heart and has not yet entered the capillaries.

148. Capillaries (page 198)
1. Capillaries enable exchange of oxygen and nutrients in the blood with carbon dioxide and wastes from the cells.
2. Capillaries are very small blood vessels forming networks that penetrate all parts of the body. The only tissue present is an endothelium of squamous epithelial cells. In contrast, arteries have a thin endothelium, a central layer of elastic tissue and smooth muscle and an outer layer of elastic and connective tissue that anchors the vessel. Veins have a thin endothelium, a central layer of elastic and muscle tissue and a relatively thick outer layer of connective tissue. Veins also have valves.
3. Blood contains a large number of all different blood cell types including erythrocytes, leucocytes, and platelets. It also has high levels of glucose, amino acids, and oxygen compared to tissue fluid and lymph. Tissue fluid contains far fewer cells than blood (only leucocytes), no glucose, low levels of amino acids and oxygen, and higher levels of carbon dioxide (produced by the cells of the tissues). Lymph is similar in composition to tissue fluid, but has more lymphocytes (a type of leucocyte). Blood and tissue fluid both contain proteins and hormones but these are absent from lymph.

149. Capillary Networks (page 199)
1. Capillary networks are branching networks of fine blood vessels where exchanges between the blood and tissues take place. Blood enters the network at the arteriolar end and is collected by venules at the venous end. The true capillaries form a vast network outside of the vascular shunt.
2. The smooth muscle sphincters regulate the blood flow to the capillary network by contracting to restrict blood flow to the network and relaxing to allow blood to flow in. The vascular shunt connects the arteriole and venule and allows blood to bypass the capillaries when the smooth muscle sphincters are contracted.
3. (a) Condition A would occur when the body is restricting blood flow to the capillaries, for example when trying to conserve heat by diverting blood away from the extremities.
   (b) Condition B would occur when the body is trying to remove excess heat by diverting blood to the skin and extremities or when the body is trying to provide extra blood to areas of high metabolism, e.g. when exercising or digesting food.
4. A portal venous system drains blood from one capillary network into another. An example is the hepatic portal system which drains blood from the capillary network in the gut lumen to the capillary network in the liver. Normally capillary networks drain into veins that return directly to the heart.

150. The Formation of Tissue Fluid (page 200)
1. The tissue fluid bathes the tissues, providing oxygen and nutrients as well as a medium for the transport (away) of metabolic wastes, e.g. CO_2.
2. Capillaries are very small blood vessels forming networks or beds that penetrate all parts of the body. Capillary walls are thin enough to allow gas exchange between the capillaries and surrounding tissue.
3. (a) Arteriolar end: Hydrostatic pressure predominates, causing water and solutes to move out of the capillaries.
   (b) Venous end: Reduction in hydrostatic pressure and the retention of proteins within the capillary tends to draw fluid back into the capillary (presence of proteins lowers the solute potential and creates an oncotic pressure, which predominates when hydrostatic pressure falls).
4. (a) Most tissue fluid finds its way directly back into the capillaries as a result of net inward pressure at the venule end of the capillary bed.
   (b) The lymph vessels (which parallel the blood system) drain tissue fluid (as lymph) back into the heart, thereby returning it into the main circulation.

151. The Human Heart (page 201)
1. (a) Pulmonary artery   (e) Aorta
    (b) Vena cava   (f) Pulmonary vein
    (c) Right atrium (RA)   (g) Left atrium (LA)
    (d) Right ventricle (RV)   (h) Left ventricle (LV)

    Tricuspid valve between RA and RV, bicuspid valve between LA and LV. The semi-lunar valves lie between LV and aorta and between RV and pulmonary artery.

2. Valves prevent the blood flowing the wrong way through the heart and help regulate filling of the chambers.

3. (a) The heart has its own coronary blood supply to meet the high oxygen demands of the heart tissue.
    (b) There must be a system within the heart muscle itself to return deoxygenated blood and waste products of metabolism back to the right atrium.

4. If blood flow to a particular part of the heart is restricted or blocked, the part of the heart muscle supplied by that vessel will die, leading to a heart attack or infarction.

5. A: arterioles   B: venules
    C: arterioles   D: capillaries

6. (a) The pressure in the pulmonary circuit must be low to prevent accumulation of fluid in the alveoli of the lungs. The systemic circuit must operate at a higher pressure in order to maintain high glomerular (kidney) filtration rates and still have the pressure to supply blood to the brain.
    (b) The left ventricle must be thicker (than the right) because it pumps blood to the systemic circuit and must develop the higher pressure required by this system. The right side of the heart has a thinner walled ventricle as it must provide a lower pressure pulmonary blood flow.

7. You are recording expansion and recoil of the artery that occurs with each contraction of the left ventricle.

152. The Cardiac Cycle (page 203)
1. (a) Aortic pressure is highest when the ventricle is contracting (ventricular pressure also maximum)
    (b) QRS wave immediately precedes increase in ventricular pressure.
    (c) The left ventricle is relaxed and filling.

2. During the period of electrical recovery the heart muscle cannot contract. This ensures that the heart has an enforced rest and will not fatigue, nor accumulate lactic acid (as occurs in working skeletal muscle).

3. Extra text removed and letters placed for each cycle.

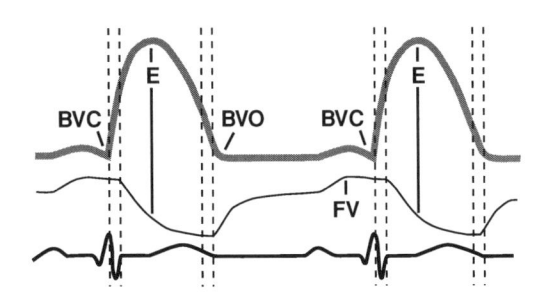

153. Dissecting a Mammalian Heart (page 204)
1. Base; Interventricular sulcus (with fat); Coronary artery

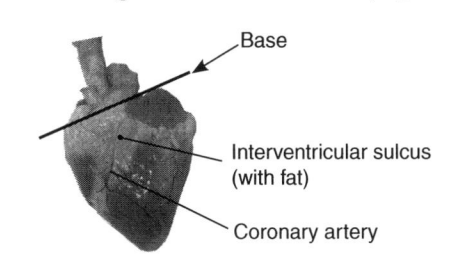

2. Vena cava

3. Aorta

4. Pulmonary artery

5. Chordae tendineae hold the valves between the atrium and ventricle closed during contraction of the ventricle.

6. The thickness of the ventricle walls (the right ventricle wall is relatively thin while the left ventricle wall is much thicker and very muscular).

154. Exercise and Heart Rate (page 206)
1. (a) The graph produced is dependent on student's own response to exercise.
    (b) Students should see an increase in both heart rate and breathing rate during the exercise period.

2. (a) After one minute of rest, students should see a decrease in both heart rate and breathing rate. After five minutes both should have decreased even further, and may have returned to pre-exercise levels.
    (b) Once exercise is completed, the body's metabolic rate falls. The demand for energy and oxygen falls, and the heart rate and breathing rate will fall accordingly.

155. Cardiovascular Disease (page 207)
1. Cardiovascular disease (CVD) refers to a class of diseases that affect the cardiovascular system (the heart or the blood vessels).

2. **Congenital CVD** refers to cardiovascular problems that are present at birth. They can be inherited, the result of viral infections, or the result of genetic defects (mutations). In contrast, **acquired CVD** describes cardiovascular diseases arising during the course of a person's life. They are mostly the result of environmental or lifestyle factors, but can sometimes be the result of genetics.

3. CVD is a major public health concern because it is so widespread (being the single most common cause of death in the UK) and costs billions of pounds in lost productivity and heath care costs. Importantly, many of the risk factors associated with CVD are preventable, so education and public health management has a role to play in reducing the levels of CVD in the population.

156. CVD Risk Factors (page 208)
1. (a) Controllable risk factors for CVD are those that can be altered by changing diet or other lifestyle factors, or by controlling a physiological disease state (e.g. high blood pressure, or high blood cholesterol). Uncontrollable risk factors are those over which no control is possible, e.g. genetic predisposition, sex, or age. Note that the impact of uncontrollable factors can be reduced by changing controllable factors.
    (b) Controllable risk factors often occur together because some tend to be causative for others, or at least always associated, e.g. obesity greatly increases the risk of high blood lipids and high blood pressure: all factors increase the risk of CVD.
    (c) Those with several risk factors have a higher chance of developing CVD because the risks are cumulative and add up to present a greater total risk.

2. (a) LDL deposits cholesterol on the endothelial lining of blood vessels, whereas HDL transports cholesterol to the liver where it is processed. A high LDL:HDL ratio is more likely to result in CVD because more cholesterol will be deposited in blood vessels and contribute to atherosclerosis.
    (b) The LDL:HDL ratio is a more accurate predictor of heart disease risk than total cholesterol *per se*, since it more accurately indicates how much cholesterol will be deposited in arteries.

3. (a) The study clearly shows that as body mass index increases there is also an increase in the risk of cardiovascular disease.
    (b) The study's strength is the large number of people included in the study.

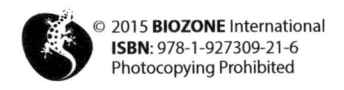

157. Reducing the Risk (page 210)
1. (a) Deaths from CHD have steadily fallen since 1970. Current levels are approximately 60% less than in 1970 (using percentage decrease formula: (older - newer) ÷ older).
   (b) Rates of smoking in adults have declined over time and are approximately half the level they were in 1970.
2. (a) There is a strong correlation between CHD deaths and smoking rates; they have been declining together since the 1970s.
   (b) No; a correlation, even a strong one, does not prove direct causation. However, the link can be made on the weight of other supporting evidence.
3. Public health education programmes present information gathered from scientific studies in a simple and easily understood way. They can help raise awareness in the public, and potentially bring about widespread change. The effectiveness of these campaigns varies; a successful campaign can take a lot of time and money, but has the potential to save millions in health care and related expenses.

158. Evaluating the Risk (page 211)
1. (a) Saturated fat consumption is generally decreasing (decreasing in the case of lard (cooking fat) and about steady for butter). Mortality for all CVD is also decreasing.
   (b) Contradicting information includes:
   - No link between red meat and CVD from Europe or Australasia
   - 2014 study finds no link between saturated fat and heart disease
   - Margaric acid (a saturated fat in milk) may actually prevent heart disease
   - Butter consumption is steady while heart disease cases are decreasing.
2. (a) The graphs do not seem to support this claim. Obesity is steadily rising while CVD mortality is steadily decreasing.
   (b) Smoking appears to be the greatest risk factor. Rates of smoking are decreasing along with CVD mortality.

159. Vascular Tissue in Plants (page 212)
1. Water
2. a) Xylem: Carries water and minerals. Mechanism: **Osmosis** (passive movement of water across a partially permeable membrane from higher to lower concentration of water molecules). Also **tension-cohesion** and (to a lesser extent) root pressure.
   (b) Phloem: Carries sugars and minerals. Mechanism: **Active transport** to load the sugar into the phloem tissue, **osmosis** (water follows sugar into the phloem), **pressure-flow** of the sap along the phloem.
3. A plant must regulate when stomata are open in order to regulate the amount of water lost by transpiration. Losing too much water will cause the plant to wilt.

160. Xylem and Phloem (page 213)
1. Xylem is strengthened by having hard fibre cells and spiral thickening of the vessel walls.
2. In gymnosperms, the only conducting cells in the xylem are tracheids, whereas the xylem of angiosperms contains both tracheids and vessel elements.
3. The perforations of the sieve plate enable the sugar solution to pass through and along the sieve tubes.
4. (a) The sieve tube.
   (b) The companion cell keeps the sieve tube cell alive and controls its activity.
5. Xylem is a dead tissue (the cells have lost the nucleus, organelles, and cytoplasm), while phloem is alive (some cells remain fully functional). Xylem transports water and dissolved minerals around the plant (from roots to leaves). Phloem conducts dissolved sugar around the plant from sources to sinks.

161. Identifying Xylem and Phloem (page 214)
1. 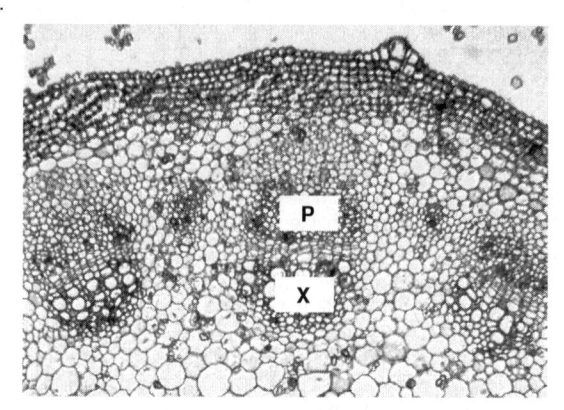
2. 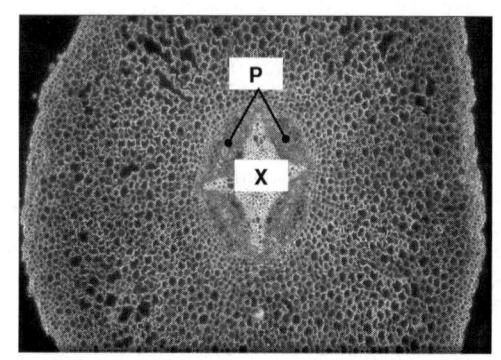
3. A: Fibre cap   D: Cortex
   B: Phloem   E: Vascular cambium
   C: Xylem   F: Pith

162. Uptake at the Root (page 215)
1. (a) Passive absorption of minerals along with the water and active transport.
   (b) Apoplastic pathway (about 90%): water moves through the xylem and the spaces within cell walls.
   Symplastic pathway: water moves through the cell cytoplasm from cell to cell via plasmodesmata.
2. Large water uptake allows plants to take up sufficient quantities of minerals from the soil. These are often in very low concentration in the soil and low water uptakes would not provide adequate quantities.
3. (a) The Casparian strip represents a barrier to water flow through the apoplast into the stele. It forces the water to move into the cells (i.e. move via the symplastic route).
   (b) This feature enables the plant to regulate ion uptake, i.e. absorb ions selectively. The movement of ions through the apoplast cannot be regulated because the flow does not occur across any partially permeable membranes.

163. Transpiration (page 216)
1. (a) The evaporative loss of water from the leaves and stem of a plant.
   (b) Any one of:
   - Transpiration stream enables plants to absorb sufficient quantities of the minerals they need (the minerals are absorbed with the water and are often in low concentration in the soil).
   - Transpiration helps cool the plant.
2. Plants must have their stomata open to exchange gases with the environment and when the stomata are open they inevitably lose water.
3. Water loss is regulated by the opening and closing of stomata.
4. (a) The plant would lose water from the cells and wilt.
   (b) During a prolonged period without water (e.g. a drought).
5. Water moves by osmosis in all cases. In any order:

AQA BIOLOGY 1 MODEL ANSWERS

(a) Transpiration pull: Photosynthesis and evaporative loss of water from leaf surfaces create higher solute concentrations (lower water concentration) in the leaf cells than elsewhere, facilitating movement of water down its concentration gradient towards the site of evaporation (stomata).
(b) Cohesion-tension: Water molecules cling together and adhere to the xylem, creating an unbroken water column through the plant. The upward pull on the water creates a tension that facilitates movement of water up the plant.
(c) Root pressure provides a weak push effect for upward water movement.

6. Water is moved up the tree by a combination of cohesion-tension, transpiration pull, and root pressure, Together these process can move water up to heights of far more than 40 m.

164. Investigating Plant Transpiration (page 218)
1. (a) Plot of data below.

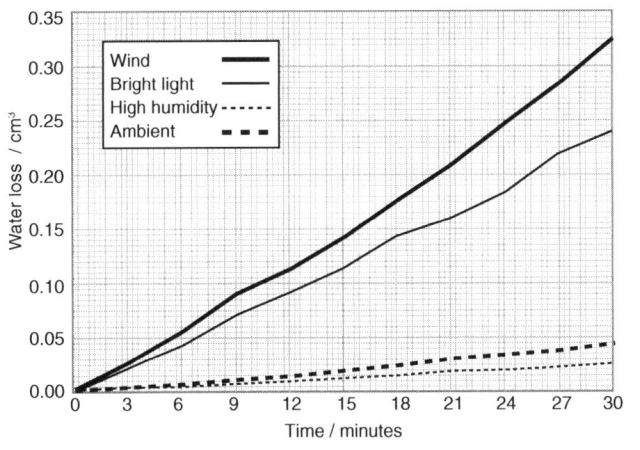

[Graph: Water loss / cm³ vs Time / minutes (0-30), showing curves for Wind, Bright light, High humidity, and Ambient]

(b) Independent variable: Time. Explanatory note: Environmental conditions are manipulated in that there are different treatments, but each condition constitutes a controlled variable (or treatment).

2. (a) Transpiration rate in ambient conditions.
(b) An experimental control enables a measure of the biological response in the absence of any of the manipulated variables being tested (no treatment). This serves as a reference point.
(c) Wind and bright light increased water loss above the ambient (control) conditions.
(d) Wind and bright light increase transpiration rate by increasing evaporative loss from the leaves. High humidity reduces transpiration rate by reducing the gradient for movement of water from leaf to air.
(e) In humid conditions, there is a reduced gradient in free water concentration between leaf and air, so the rate of diffusion of water vapour from the leaf to the environment will be slower.

165. Translocation (page 220)
1. (a) The increase in dissolved sugar in the sieve tube cell lowers the water potential. Water then moves into the sieve tube cells by osmosis, creating a pressure that pushes the sugar solution through the phloem.
(b) This means the sugar flows from its site of production (leaves) to its site of unloading (roots).

2. Food is manufactured in one region of the plant (the leaves) but is required in other regions (e.g. the roots and fruits). It must be transported there.

3. (a) Translocation: The transport (around the plant) of the organic products of photosynthesis.
(b) The bulk movement of phloem sap along a gradient in hydrostatic pressure (generated osmotically).
(c) The coupling of sucrose transport (into the transfer cell) to the diffusion of H⁺ down a concentration gradient (generated by a proton pump).

4. Sucrose is transported into the phloem by a protein symport. Sucrose is coupled to diffusion of hydrogen ions into the cell.
5. The transfer cell uses active transport mechanisms (coupled transport of sucrose) to accumulate sucrose to levels 2-3 times those in the mesophyll. The sucrose then moves into the sieve tube cell.
6. (a) The flow of phloem indicates the phloem stream is under pressure.
(b) The greatest flow rate would be nearest the source (leaves) as this would have the greatest concentration of sugars.
(c) The stylets penetrate the phloem precisely and without damage. Aphids feeding on different parts of the plant can be used to measure flow rates.

166. Experimental Evidence for Plant Transport (page 222)
1. The ringing experiment shows the phloem is under pressure. It also shows the phloem carries nutrients as growth above the ring is not impeded.
2. It shows that sugars are transported from the leaves to other parts of the plant, but not other leaves.
3. The mass flow hypothesis assumes all fluid in the phloem is moving in the same direction. If some solutes are moving in opposite directions a new hypothesis would be needed to account for this.
4. If sap moved by pressure-flow, then there should be selective pressure for the sieve plate to be lost or become less of a barrier, yet this has not happened. Of course, there are also selective pressures that operate against loss of the sieve plate, such as the need to have discrete yet freely communicating cells.

167. Chapter Review (page 223)
No model answer. Summary is the student's own.

168. KEY TERMS: Did You Get it? (page 225)
1. (a) and (b)

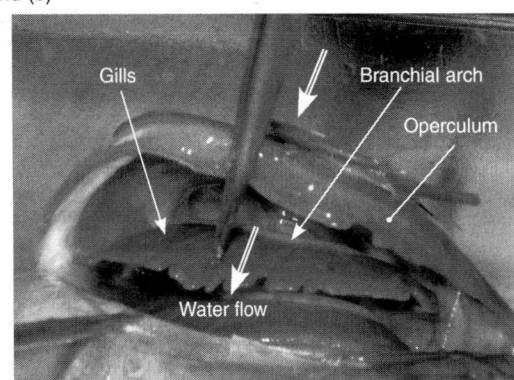

[Image of fish gill dissection with labels: Gills, Branchial arch, Operculum, Water flow]

(c) The fish opens its mouth and water enters. The operculum bulges letting the water move to the opercular cavity. The mouth closes and the operculum opens, moving water out past the gills.

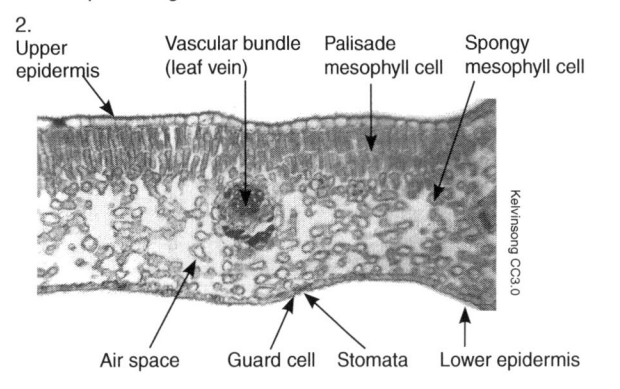

2. [Image of leaf cross-section with labels: Upper epidermis, Vascular bundle (leaf vein), Palisade mesophyll cell, Spongy mesophyll cell, Air space, Guard cell, Stomata, Lower epidermis]

© 2015 BIOZONE International
ISBN: 978-1-927309-21-6
Photocopying Prohibited

3. alveoli (L), countercurrent flow (I), expiration (H), gas exchange (E), gills (F), haemoglobin (K), inspiration (M), lungs (J), oxyhaemoglobin dissociation curve (A), respiratory gas (G), respiratory pigment (B), spiracles (C), stomata (D)

4. (a) Artery (b) Vein (c) Capillary

5. (a) Systole (b) Diastole

6. (a) An ECG or electrocardiogram

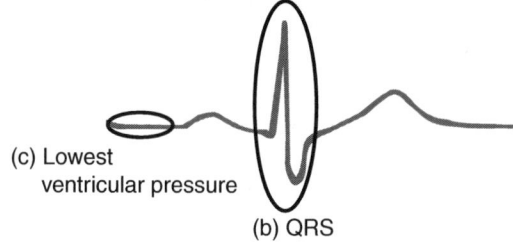

   (c) Lowest ventricular pressure
   (b) QRS
   (d) Ventricular volume is increasing

7. (a) Transpiration (or evapotranspiration)
   (b) Xylem
   (c) Dead
   (d) No

8. (a) Sieve tube end plate
   (b) Phloem
   (c) Alive
   (d) Translocation or transport of sugars
   (e) Sugar or sucrose in solution

9. artery (K), atrium (J), blood (C), capillary (E), cardiac cycle (B), cohesion-tension hypothesis (M), heart (F), phloem (G), sink (H), source (I), vein (L), ventricle (D), xylem (A)

169. Prokaryotic Chromosomes (page 229)

1. (a)-(c) any of in any order:
   - The prokaryotic chromosome is a singular circular chromosome. Eukaryote chromosomes comprise linear DNA packaged with proteins.
   - In prokaryotes, some genes are carried on extra-chromosomal plasmid DNA.
   - The prokaryote chromosome is attached to the plasma membrane and is not enclosed in a nuclear membrane (unlike eukaryotic chromosomes).
   - Prokaryotic chromosomes consists almost entirely of protein coding genes and their regulatory sequences. Eukaryotic chromosomes contain much intronic DNA that does not code for proteins.

2. Because the DNA in prokaryotes is in direct contact with the cytoplasm, transcription (making mRNA) and translation (protein synthesis) can occur at the same time and the entire process of gene expression occurs much more rapidly than in eukaryotic cells, where the mRNA must leave the nucleus and enter the cytoplasm before translation can begin.

3. Question shuld read " What is the consequence of this to the relative sizes of bacterial and eukaryotic **genomes**".
   The bacterial genome (chromosome) is much smaller than the eukaryotic genome (all chromosomes).

170. Eukaryote Chromosome Structure (page 230)

1. In the nucleus

2. The DNA molecule is very large. Without packaging it up it would be difficult to fit the DNA into the cell nucleus, especially during replication and mitosis.

3. DNA wraps around the histone proteins, taking up less space that if it was spread out.

4. (a) **DNA**: A long, complex nucleic acid molecule found in the chromosomes of nearly all organisms (some viruses have RNA instead). Provides the genetic instructions for producing proteins and other gene products (e.g. RNAs).
   (b) **Chromatin**: Chromosomal material consisting of DNA, RNA, and histone and non-histone proteins. The term refers to chromosomes in the non-condensed state.
   (c) **Nucleosome**: The basic unit of DNA packing consisting of a length of DNA wrapped around a bead of 8 histones.
   (d) **Chromatid**: One copy of a newly replicated chromosome, which is joined to the other copy at the centromere.

5. Exons are protein-coding regions of DNA. Introns are non-protein coding regions of DNA. Introns are excised from the primary transcript mRNA to form the mature mRNA.

6. Both mitochondria and chloroplasts have circular DNA without introns. The DNA in mitochondria and chloroplasts is replicated independently of the nucleus. The DNA in mitochondria and chloroplasts is not associated with proteins.

171. Genomes (page 232)

1. (a) 49.67 times bigger
   (b) 652.2 times smaller
   (c) 18 750 times smaller

2. Large genomes require a lot of resources to replicate, thus reproduction and growth rates are low and this increases the risk of extinction.

172. The Genetic Code (page 233)

1. This exercise demonstrates the need for a 3-nucleotide sequence for each codon and the resulting degeneracy in the genetic code.

Amino acid	Codons						No.
Alanine	GCU	GCC	GCA	GCG			4
Arginine	CGU	CGC	CGA	CGG	AGA	AGG	6
Asparagine	AAU	AAC					2
Aspartic Acid	GAU	GAC					2
Cysteine	UGU	UGC					2
Glutamine	CAA	CAG					2
Glutamic Acid	GAA	GAG					2
Glycine	GGU	GGC	GGA	GGG			4
Histidine	CAU	CAC					2
Isoleucine	AUU	AUC	AUA				3
Leucine	UAA	UUG	CUU	CUC	CUA	CUG	6
Lysine	AAA	AAG					2
Methionine	AUG						1
Phenylalanine	UUU	UUC					2
Proline	CCU	CCC	CCA	CCG			4
Serine	UCU	UCC	UCA	UCG	AGU	AGC	6
Threonine	ACU	ACC	ACA	ACG			4
Tryptophan	UGG						1
Tyrosine	UAU	UAC					2
Valine	GUU	GUC	GUA	GUG			4

2. (a) 16 amino acids
   (b) Two-base codons (e.g. AT, GG, CG, TC, CA) do not give enough combinations with the 4-base alphabet (A, T, G and C) to code for the 20 amino acids.

3. Many of the codons for a single amino acid vary in the last base only. This would reduce the effect of point mutations, creating new and potentially harmful amino acid sequences in only some instances. **Note**: Only 61 codons are displayed above. The remaining three are **terminator** (STOP) codons. These are considered the 'punctuation' or controlling codons that mark the end of a gene sequence. The amino acid **methionine** (AUG) is regarded as the 'start' (initiator) codon.

173. DNA Carries the Code (page 234)

1. Griffith first injected disease causing bacteria into healthy mice to confirm the action of the bacteria. The bacteria were then heated to kill them and injected into healthy mice. These mice did not develop pneumonia confirming it was the living bacteria that was causing the disease.

2. Sulfur is found in proteins but not in DNA (or to a much lesser extent) while phosphorus is found in DNA but not proteins. If the sulfur was found in the infected bacteria then the proteins carried the genetic information. If phosphorus was found then it was the DNA that carried the information.

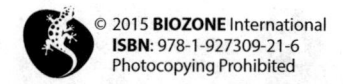

AQA BIOLOGY 1 MODEL ANSWERS

3. This shows that the result is not peculiar to, or the result of, the experiment itself. Rather it is a property of the system being studied.

174. Genes to Proteins (page 235)
1. (a) A triplet   (b) A codon

2. (a) A gene is a section of DNA that codes for a protein. it is the functional unit of heredity.
   (b) RNA polymerase.
   (c) The promoter acts as a region for the RNA polymerase to bind to to start transcription. A terminator indicates where RNA polymerase should stop transcribing.

3. Gene expression is the process of rewriting a gene into a protein. It involves two stages, transcription and translation.

4. Transcription and translation occur only in 5' to 3' direction (polymerases work only 5' to 3' because the OH on the 3' is the active site for forming the phosphodiester bond).

175. Transcription (page 236)
1. (a) to (c) in any order:
   - Transcription in prokaryotes can happen at the same time as translation (both happen in the cytoplasm).
   - Transcription in eukaryotes occurs in the nucleus.
   - Transcription in eukaryotes produces a primary mRNA, which is then 'edited' to produce a mature mRNA.
   - In prokaryotes, the RNA polymerase bind directly to the promoter region of the DNA.

2. In prokaryotes, translation (producing the protein) can occur at the same time as transcription, so the process is very rapid. In addition, the mRNA requires no editing (no need to splice exons together).

3. The template strand.

4. Complementary means that the bases on mRNA will match up with those on the DNA template strand according to the base pairing rule. In the case of DNA - RNA bases matching, A is matched with U, T with A, C with G, and G with C.

5. mRNA carries a copy of the genetic instructions from the DNA (master instructions) to ribosomes in the cytoplasm. The rate of protein synthesis can be increased by making many copies of identical mRNA from the same piece of DNA.

6. (a) AUG
   (b) UAA, UAG, UGA

7. (a) AUG AUC GGC GCU AAA
   (b) AUG UUC GGA UAU UUU

8. Mature RNA has had the intron sections found in the primary mRNA removed. It consists only of exons.

176. Translation (page 238)
1. AUG AUC GGC GCU AAA

2. (a) 61
   (b) There are 64 possible codons for mRNA, but three are terminator codons. 61 codons for mRNA require 61 tRNAs each with a complementary codon.

177. Protein Synthesis Summary (page 239)
1. (a) 1: Unwinding the DNA molecule.
   (b) 2: mRNA synthesis: Nucleotides added to the growing strand of messenger RNA molecule.
   (c) 3: DNA rewinds into double helix structure.
   (d) 4: mRNA moves through nuclear pore in nuclear membrane to the cytoplasm.
   (e) 5: tRNA molecule brings in the correct amino acid to the ribosome.
   (f) 6: Anti-codon on the bottom of the tRNA matches with the correct codon on the mRNA and drops off the amino acid.
   (g) 7: tRNA leaves the ribosome.
   (h) 8: tRNA molecule is recharged with another amino acid, ready to participate in protein synthesis.

2. (a) DNA   (f) Nuclear pore
   (b) Free nucleotides   (g) tRNA
   (c) RNA polymerase enzyme (h) Amino acids
   (d) mRNA   (i) Ribosome
   (e) Nuclear membrane   (j) Polypeptide chain

3. (a) Whether or not the protein is required by the cell (regulated by control of gene expression).
   (b) Whether or not there is an adequate pool of the amino acids and tRNAs required for the particular protein in question.

178. Gene Mutations and Mutagens (page 240)
1. A **frame shift mutation** occurs when the sequence of bases is offset by one position (by adding or deleting a base). This alters the order in which the bases are grouped as triplets and can severely alter the amino acid sequence.

2. (a) Reading frame shifts and nonsense substitutions.
   (b) They may cause large scale disruption of the coded instructions for making a protein. Either a completely wrong amino acid sequence for part of the protein or a protein that is partly completed (missing amino acids due to an out-of-place terminator codon).
   (c) A substitution mutation to the third base in a codon. Because of degeneracy in the genetic code, a substitution at the third base position may not change the amino acid that is encoded.

3. (a) Mutated DNA: AAA ATA TTT CTC CAA GAT
       mRNA: UUU UAU AAA GAG GUU CUA
       Amino acids: Phe Tyr Lys Glu Val Leu
   (b) ATG → UAC →Tyr = Tyrosine
   (c) No effect because of code degeneracy; both UAC and UAU code for Tyr.

4. Somatic mutations occur in the body (non-gametic or somatic) cells and are not inherited. They may affect an individual within its lifetime. Gametic mutations are mutations to the gametes (in testes or ovaries) and are inherited. Gametic mutations are inherited. They are passed on to the next generation and can become part of the genetic variation in the gene pool (upon which natural selection can act).

5. (a) Radiation: Ultraviolet (UV) rays from the sun, X-rays from medical equipment, gamma-rays from medical equipment and nuclear contamination.
   (b) Chemicals: Benzene, formalin (formaldehyde), carbon tetrachloride.

6. A mutagen increases the frequency of mutation (change or disruption in DNA) above the spontaneous (background) rate. Mutagens bring about their effects by disrupting the base sequence of genes, which can affect that gene's product. Mutations to regulatory genes, such as those controlling cell division, are among the most damaging.

179. Meiosis (page 242)
1. In the first division of meiosis, homologous pairs of chromosomes pair to form bivalents. Segments of chromosome may be exchanged in crossing over and the homologues then separate (are pulled apart). This division reduces the number of chromosomes in the intermediate cells, so that only one chromosome from each homologous pair is present.

2. In the second division of meiosis, chromatids separate (are pulled apart), but the number of chromosomes stays the same. This is more or less a 'mitotic' division.

3. (a) DNA replication occurs in interphase.
   (b) A chromosome is a single piece of coiled, condensed DNA. A chromatid is one half of a replicated chromosome (held to its other chromatid at the centromere).

4. (a) A haploid cell has only one set of chromosomes. A diploid cell has two sets of chromosomes.
   (b) The haploid cells are at the bottom of the diagram (the gametes).

5. (a) ABCD   (c) abcD
   (b) ABCd   (d) abcd

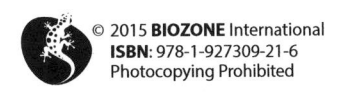

6. (a) Unexpected combinations of alleles for genes will be present in gametes (recombinants).
   (b) The offspring are more genetically variable than they would otherwise be.

180. Crossing Over Problems (page 244)
Each problem stands alone (they are not a sequence).

1. (a) Gene sequences after crossing over at point 2:

   ```
   2
   a b c d e f g   h i j k l m n o p  1
   A B C d e f g   h i j k l m n o p  2
   a b c D E F G   H I J K L M N O P  3
   A B C D E F G   H I J K L M N O P  4
   ```

   (b) A, B and C

2. (a) Gene sequences after crossing over at points 6 & 7:

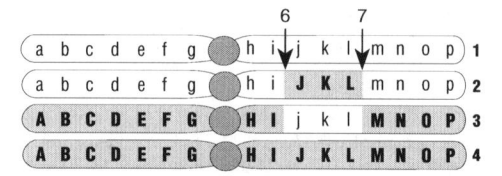

   ```
         6     7
   a b c d e f g   h i j k l m n o p  1
   a b c d e f g   h i J K L m n o p  2
   A B C D E F G   H I j k l M N O P  3
   A B C D E F G   H I J K L M N O P  4
   ```

   (b) J, K and L

3. (a) Gene sequences after crossing over at points 1 and 3, 5 and 7. (Note that results for chromatids 2 & 3 are interchangeable):

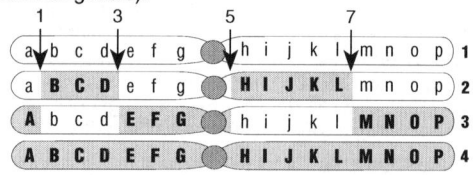

   ```
   1   3       5     7
   a b c d e f g   h i j k l m n o p  1
   a B C D e f g   H I J K L m n o p  2
   A b c d E F G   h i j k l M N O P  3
   A B C D E F G   H I J K L M N O P  4
   ```

   (b) B, C, D and H, I, J, K, L

4. Genes on one chromosome would be inherited together and there would be less variation in the gametes and therefore in the offspring. Variation would arise only from mutation and from the combination of maternal and paternal gametes at fertilisation.

181. Modelling Meiosis (page 245)
The genotype/phenotype of the offspring students obtain will depend on their own phenotypes.

182. Mitosis vs Meiosis (page 247)
1. Mitosis involves a division of the chromatids into two new daughter cells thus maintaining the original number of chromosomes in the parent cell. Meiosis involves a division of the homologous pairs of chromosomes into two intermediary daughter cells thus reducing the diploid number by half. The second stage of meiosis is similar to a mitotic division, but the haploid number is maintained because the chromatids separate.

2. The first meiotic division is a reduction division, halving the number of chromosomes. The second division is a 'mitotic' type division, the chromatids are separated but the number of chromosomes remain the same.

3. The processes of recombination and independent assortment of the chromosomes during meiosis sort alleles into different combinations and thus introduces genetic diversity.

183. Non-Disjunction in Meiosis (page 248)
1. Non-disjunction results in abnormal gamete numbers in some gametes. As a result, certain phenotypic traits are exhibited (e.g. facial features, mental retardation).Certain metabolic processes may also be affected.

2. Non-disjunction in the parental cell during meiosis I results in both the daughter cells being faulty which will be transferred to the daughter cells produced in meiosis II. Nondisjunction in a parental cell during meiosis II results in only half the total number of daughter cells being faulty.

3. The maternal age effect refers to an increased risk of chromosome abnormalities with advancing maternal age. The risk of aneuploidies, such as Down syndrome, increase with every year a women ages.

184. Meiosis and Life Cycles (page 249)
1. (a) 2N   (d) Fertilisation
   (b) N   (e) Mitosis
   (c) Meiosis

2. The prothallus

3. Meiosis produces spores.

4. Meiosis occurs in the sex organs (ovaries and testes) and produces germ cells or gametes.

185. Mechanism of Natural Selection (page 250)
1. 1) Overproduction of the population, 2) genetic variation in the population, 3) competition for resources and survival of those with more favourable variations (natural selection), 4) inheritance of favourable variations and proliferation of individuals with these variations.

2. Mutations (creates new alleles) and sexual reproduction (produces new combinations of alleles).

3. The changes in the inherited characteristics of a population over generations.

4. A population produces more offspring than will survive to reproduce. There is genetic variation in the offspring. Some of this variation will result in offspring phenotypes that are more suited to the prevailing environment than others. Competition will select for favourable phenotypes. The genetic component of the variation will be inherited by the next generation so that proportionally more of the favourable phenotype will be present in the next generation of offspring. Over time, favourable phenotypes will proliferate and unfavourable phenotypes will become rare or disappear.

5.

Beetle population	% Brown beetle	% Red beetles	% Red beetles with spots
1	86.7	6.7	6.7
2	46.6	33.3	20
3	20	46.7	33.3

186. Types of Natural Selection (page 252)
1. (a) Stable
   (b) Stable environments favour the most common phenotypes. In a stable environment, it is unlikely that extreme phenotypes will be adaptive, so selection acts to prevent a divergence from what is 'already working'. Predictability encourages a reduction in phenotypic variability because this is no disadvantage when the environment is static.

2. (a) Changing.
   (b) Environmental change, especially trending in one direction, selects for phenotypes with higher fitness in the new conditions. The most common phenotype no longer shows the highest fitness and the phenotypic norm shifts.

3. (a) Drought favoured birds with beak sizes at two extremes of the range, since these birds could exploit the small and the large seed sizes.

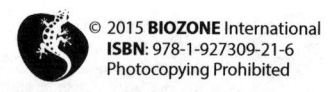

(b) The selection pressures favouring a bimodal distribution in beak size would be reduced and medium sized beaks would become relatively more common.

187. The Evolution of Antibiotic Resistance (page 253)
1. Antibiotic resistance refers to the resistance bacteria show to antibiotics that would normally inhibit their growth. In other words, they no longer show a reduction in growth response in the presence of the antibiotic.
2. (a) Antibiotic resistance arises in a bacterial population as result of mutation.
   (b) Resistance can become widespread as a result of (1) transfer of genetic material between bacteria (horizontal gene transfer) or by (2) increasing resistance with each generation a result of natural selection processes (vertical evolution).
3. Methicillin resistant *Staphylococcus aureus* (MRSA) have acquired genes for resistance to penicillin and related antibiotics, so these antibiotics are no longer effective against MRSA. This is a problem because S. aureus infections are very common and they are becoming more difficult to treat and control. If resistance continues to develop, there may be no way of treating them in the future.

188. Measuring Antibiotic Sensitivity (page 254)
1. (a) Antibiotic A is the most effective antibiotic because it produced the largest zone of clearance.
   (b) Disc 3
   (c) It achieved the same result as disc 4 but at a lower concentration.

189. Selection For Human Birth Weight (page 255)

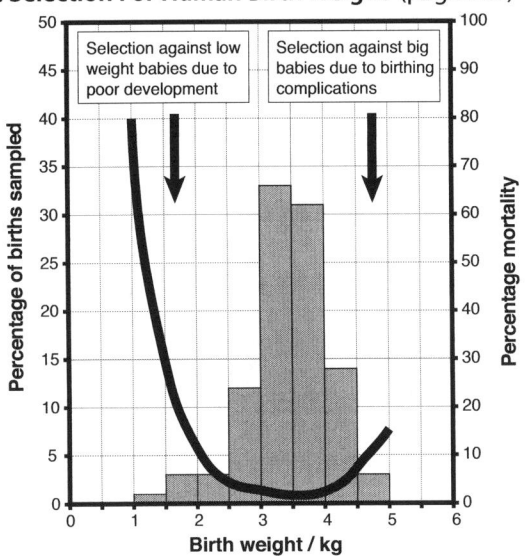

Note: For the construction of weight classes, it is necessary to have a range of weight categories that do not overlap. The data collected should be sorted into weight classes of: 0.0-0.49, 0.50-0.99, 1.0-1.49, 1.5-1.99, etc.

Sample data: Use the data below if students are unable to collect from local sources.

3.740	3.830	3.530	3.095	3.630
1.560	3.910	4.180	3.570	2.660
3.150	3.400	3.380	2.660	3.375
3.840	3.630	3.810	2.640	3.955
2.980	3.350	3.780	3.260	4.510
3.800	4.170	4.400	3.770	3.400
3.825	3.130	3.400	3.260	4.100
3.220	3.135	3.090	3.830	3.970
3.840	4.710	4.050	4.560	3.350
3.380	3.690	1.495	3.260	3.430
3.510	3.230	3.570	3.620	3.260
3.315	3.230	3.790	2.620	3.030
3.350	3.970	3.915	2.040	4.050
3.105	3.790	3.060	2.770	3.400
1.950	3.800	2.390	2.860	4.110
1.970	3.800	4.490	2.640	3.550
4.050	4.220	2.860	4.060	3.740
4.082	3.000	3.230	2.800	4.050
4.300	3.030	3.160	3.300	2.350
3.970	2.980	3.550	3.070	2.715

1. Normal distribution (bell-shaped curve), probably with a skew to the left.
2. 3.5 kg (taken from the table: only 2% mortality)
3. Good correlation. Lowest frequencies of surviving birth weights correspond to birth weights of highest mortality.
4. Selection pressures operate at extremes of the range: premature babies have reduced survival because their body systems are not fully developed; large babies present problems with delivery as the birth canal can only accommodate babies up to a certain size. **Note**: Very large babies can occur as the result of gestational diabetes. Before adequate medical intervention, this often led to the death of the mother and/or the baby.
5. Medical intervention can now allow babies that are very premature to survive (babies as small as 1.5 kg have a good chance of survival today, but this has not historically been the case). Caesarean deliveries have also allowed larger babies to be born. **Note**: This technology is available to wealthy societies thereby reducing the effect of this selection pressure. Developing countries still experience this selection pressure.

190. Observing Natural Selection (page 256)
1. (a)

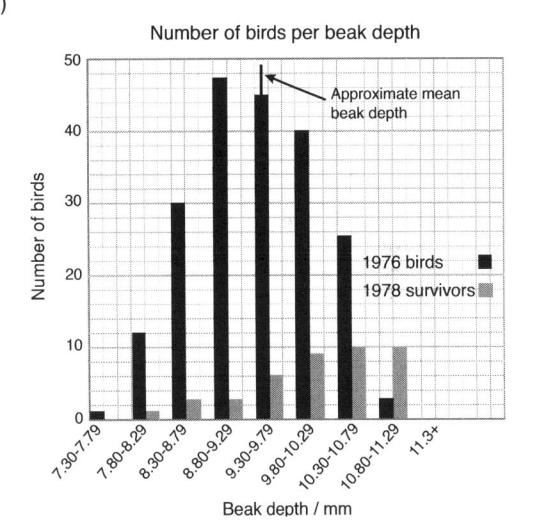

   (b)

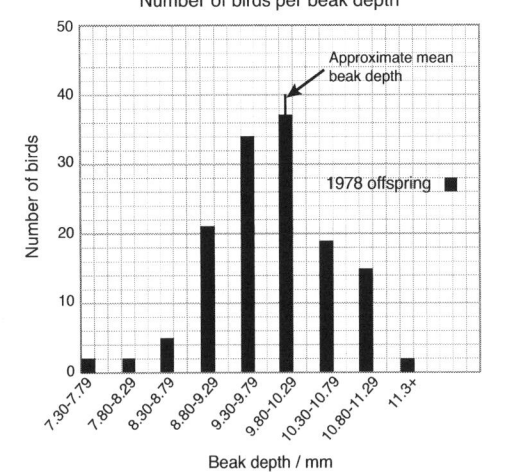

2. Directional selection

3. (a) See graphs above.
   (b) Approximately 0.5 mm
   (c) Yes, beak depth is heritable. If the drought continues the population may become increasingly dominated by individuals with deeper beaks. Smaller beak sizes will become increasingly rare or absent.

4. Smaller seeds were probably eaten first (as beaks were smaller). This left the birds competing for larger seeds such that birds with larger beaks were more successful and were more likely to survive.

191. Adaptations and Fitness (page 257)
Note rhino photo labels mistakenly transposed (since corrected).

1. Adaptive features are genetically determined traits that have a function to the organism in its environment. Acclimatisation refers to the changes made by an organism during its lifetime to environmental conditions (note that some adaptive features do involve changes in physiology).

2. Shorter extremities are associated with colder climates, whereas elongated extremities are associated with warmer climates. The differences are associated with heat conservation (shorter limbs/ears lose less heat to the environment).

3. Large body sizes conserve more heat and have more heat producing mass relative to the surface area over which heat is lost.

4. **Snow bunting** adaptations:
   (a) **Structural**: Large amount of white plumage reduces heat loss, white feathers are hollow and air filled (acting as good insulators).
   (b) **Physiological**: Lay one or two more eggs than (ecologically) equivalent species further south producing larger broods (improving breeding success), rapid moult to winter plumage is suited to the rapid seasonal changes of the Arctic.
   (c) **Behavioural**: Feeding activity continues almost uninterrupted during prolonged daylight hours (allowing large broods to be raised and improving survival and breeding success), migration to overwintering regions during Arctic winter (escapes harsh Arctic winter), will burrow into snow drifts for shelter (withstand short periods of very bad weather), males assist in brood rearing (improved breeding success).

5. Extra detail is (italics) provided as explanation:
   (a) Structural (*larger, stouter body conserves heat*).
   (b) Physiological (*concentrated urine conserves water*).
   (c) Behavioural (*move to favourable sites*).
   (d) Physiological (*higher photosynthetic rates and water conservation*).
   (e) Structural (*reduction in water loss*).
   (f) Behavioural and physiological (*hibernation involves both a reduction in metabolic rate and the behaviour necessary to acquire more food before hibernation and to seek out an appropriate site*).
   (g) Behavioural (*increase in body temperature*).

192. The Biological Species Concept (page 259)
1. Behavioural (they show no interest in each other).

2. Physical barrier; sea separating Australia from SE Asia.

3. The red wolf is rare and may have difficulty finding another member of its species to mate with.

4. The populations on the two land masses, which have identical appearance and habitat requirements, were connected relatively recently by a land bridge during the last ice age (about 18,000 years ago). This would have permitted breeding between the populations. Individuals from the current populations have been brought together and are able to interbreed and produce fertile offspring.

5. Several definitions of a biological species are possible. Most simply, a species is the lowest taxonomic grouping of organisms. From a functional point of view, a species is a group of organisms that are freely interbreeding (or potentially so) but reproductively isolated from other such groups. Species are usually (but now not exclusively) recognised by their morphological characters. Cryptic species are apparently indistinguishable, but reproductively isolated as a result of behavioural or other differences. "Species" that do not reproduce sexually (with the combination of gametes) at any stage provide problems for a standard species definition. Such organisms include bacteria, where genera and 'species' are distinguished on the basis of structure and metabolism. In many cases, species are really types or strains.

193. The Phylogenetic Species Concept (page 260)
1. (a) Under the PSC, species are assigned on the basis of shared derived characteristics, which may be morphological or biochemical. A species is the smallest group that all share a derived character state.
   (b) Problems (one of):
      It can lead to a proliferation of species that are difficult to distinguish.
      It is difficult to justify its application to morphologically distinct but interbreeding populations.
   (c) The PSC might be more appropriate than the BSC for extinct organisms, and for asexually reproducing organisms such as bacteria.

2. Genetic techniques can be used to trace the occurrence of new character states and distinguish species on the basis of a unique combination of characters. Taxa that share more derived characters are more closely related than those that share fewer. This produces a hierarchy of shared character states, which leads to a tree of relatedness.

194. Behaviour and Species Recognition (page 261)
1. (a) Courtship behaviour is a means of assessing the suitability, quality, and readiness of a mate and an effective way of ensuring reproductive isolation. It also has a role in reducing natural intraspecific aggression in the potential mate.
   (b) Stereotypical behaviours are easily recognised and will elicit appropriate (and equally recognisable) behaviours in the prospective mate.

2. Effective courtship provides a way to ensure that species do not mistakenly waste resources by mating with another species. This helps to ensure the production of viable offspring and maintains the integrity of the species gene pool.

195. Classification System (page 262)
1. (a) 1. Kingdom   (b) 1. Animal
       2. Phylum   2. Chordata
       3. Class   3. Mammalia
       4. Order   4. Primates
       5. Family (given)   5. Hominidae (given)
       6. Genus   6. *Homo*
       7. Species   7. *sapiens*

2. There are many possibilities. Common examples are:
   Keep **P**ond **C**lean **O**r **F**roggy **G**ets **S**ick
   Kids **P**laying **C**ricket **O**r **F**ootball **G**et **S**marter

3. (a) Binomial nomenclature
   (b) Genus and species (generic and specific name).

4. (1) Avoid confusion over the use of common names for organisms, (2) provide a unique name for each type of organism, (3) attempt to determine/define the evolutionary relationship of organisms (phylogeny).

5. Some species can be morphologically similar and can therefore be very difficult to distinguish. The similarity may not be related to ancestry. It may be instead be related to evolution in similar environments (i.e. experiencing similar selection pressures and therefore having similar adaptations).

AQA BIOLOGY 1 MODEL ANSWERS

196. Biodiversity (page 264)
1. Species diversity refers to the number of different species within an area (species richness), while genetic diversity describes the diversity of genes within a particular species. Biodiversity is defined as the measure of all genes, species, and ecosystems in a region, so both genetic and species diversity are important in evaluating total biodiversity.

2. Different species have different habitat preferences, so within a larger heterogeneous region, a variety of different habitats can potentially can support a greater species diversity.

3. (a) Species richness measures the number of species within an ecosystem, whereas species evenness describes how equably the species are distributed within an ecosystem.
   (b) Both measures are important when considering species conservation. Species richness could give an indication of ecosystem stability, and therefore how at-risk particular species may be. Species evenness provides an indication of the species distribution (a limited distribution or a distribution where individuals are widely separated may indicate the species is at risk).

4. Keystone species are pivotal to some important ecosystem function such as production of biomass or nutrient recycling. Because their role is disproportionately large, their removal has a similarly disproportionate effect on ecosystem function.

5. **Grey wolf**: Wolves, as a top predator, are an integral component of the ecosystems to which they belong. The wide range of habitats in which they thrive reflects their adaptability as a species. Their diet includes elk, caribou, moose, deer and other large ungulates, as well as smaller prey. Wolves are sensitive to fluctuations in prey abundance, and the balance between wolves and their prey preserves the ecological balance between large herbivores and available forage.

   European beaver: When beavers build dams, many species, some of which may be threatened, benefit. As well as creating habitat, beaver ponds encourage the growth of aquatic vegetation and also result in increases in invertebrate populations. This in turn provides an enhanced food source for fish, amphibians and birds, which also benefits predators higher up the food chain (e.g. otters and grey herons), which eat the fish. Beavers are entirely herbivorous and their activity is closely tied to the regeneration of deciduous woodland tree species, including aspen, birch, oak, and rowan. Beavers eat the bark of these trees and, by harvesting the trees, promote regeneration and stand replacement.

   Scots pine: The Scots pine has relationships with many organisms. Some are associated directly with the pine itself, particularly epiphytic lichens, mosses, and mycorrhizal fungi, including the chanterelle and the extremely rare greenfoot tooth fungus. Scots pine provides habitat for a number of plant species with restricted distribution, including blaeberries and cowberries, which play a successional role in the development of the hummocks characteristic of the Scots pinewood ecosystems. A wide variety of invertebrate, mammal, and bird species, some of which are endemic and/or endangered, are also dependent directly or indirectly on the Scots pine (e.g. for habitat or food).

197. Sampling Populations (page 266)
1. We sample populations in order to gain information about their abundance and composition. Sampling is necessary because, in most cases, populations are too large to examine in total.

2. Random sampling removes bias which may influence the result of the study.

3. (a) The population is divided into mutually exclusive groups and therefore effectively separate groups (e.g. male and female). Random sampling can be applied to each group; effectively there are two separate sampling events.
   (b) Stratified sampling often occurs in large scale surveys, e.g political opinion polls, identifying differences in suburban, semi-rural, and rural populations.

4. (a) A student might use the school roll and select every 4th person on the roll, or select every 3rd person in every classroom roll.
   (b) A student might divide the school students into males and females or into year groups, before conducting a random survey.
   (c) The student may stop students in the hall between classes or at lunch break to gather information.

198. Interpreting Samples (page 267)
1. (a) The pH decreases
   (b) The increase in plant cover helps maintain moisture at ground level. Loss of organic matter from the plants (e.g. fallen leaves) add to the organic matter (humus). Moisture increases sharply at the wet slack due to the sheltered position between the dunes and the water table being close to the surface.

2. (a) 0.4 m
   (b) Lichens (various species).
   (c) Most mosses need higher moisture and lower light and temperatures than lichens.

199. Diversity Indices (page 268)
1. (a) 7 + 10 + 11 + 2 + 4 + 3 = 37. 37 x 36 = 1332. (7x6) + (10x9) + (11x10) + (2x1) + (4x3) + (3x2) = 262. 1332 / 262 = **5.08**
   (b) 16 + 4 + 1 + 3 + 4 + 2 = 30. 30 x 29 = 870. (16x4) + (4x3) + (1x0) + (3x2) + (4x3) + (2x1) = 272. 870 / 272 = **3.20**
   (c) The forest floor community is more diverse that the one near the forest margin.

200. Investigating Biodiversity (page 269)
1. Systematic

2. (a) An appropriate size of sampling unit enables you to sample the organisms effectively and collect enough data for the samples to be representative of the population(s) involved, without extra, unnecessary data collection.
   (b) Making some reasonable assumptions allows you to focus on the questions that you really want to answer and offer plausible explanations if your results do not support your predictions. It also allows you to recognise the limitations of the investigation.
   (c) Apart from standard moral obligations to do no damage, consideration of the environment is essential to being able to justify any repeat of your work, and to ensure that any repeat takes place in the same system. For the investigation to be relevant it must be carried in a relevant environment using an appropriate sampling technique.
   (d) Organisms should always be returned to the same area to avoid introducing new organisms into regions where they may previously have been absent, and to minimise the impact of sampling on the area being investigated. This is especially important if sampling is to occur on many different occasions (e.g. annually).
   (e) The sample area must cover all the possible locations that the organisms might be as to remove any bias towards a particular habitat. The total area sampled should also be appropriate to the size of the organism(s) being sampled and the questions being asked. Example: In a study of altitudinal zonation, a very short transect in a small area would not be representative of community changes.

3. (a) Site 1

Species	Number of animals	n-1	n(n-1)
1	35	34	1190
2	14	13	182
3	13	12	156
4	12	11	132
5	8	7	56
6	6	5	30
7	6	5	30
8	4	3	12
		Σn(n-1) =	1788

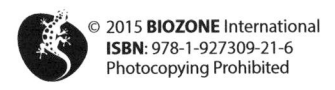

Site 2

Species	Number of animals	n-1	n(n-1)
1	74	73	5402
2	16	15	240
3	4	3	12
4	2	1	2
5	2	1	2
6	1	0	0
7	0	0	0
8	1	0	0
			$\Sigma n(n-1) = 5766$

(b) 98 × 97 = 9506 / 1788 = 5.31
(c) 100 × 99 = 9900 / 5794 = 1.72
(d) The diversity of the oak wood is greater than that of the pine plantations. This may be because the oak wood is likely to have a greater variety of plant species and that oak leaves decompose more readily than those of conifer trees, providing a greater leaf litter habitat.

201. Agriculture and Biodiversity (page 271)

1. (a) High yields are maintained by intensive farming even though some areas are retired from production.
   (b) There is a financial incentive if certain areas are left as conservation estate (income from tourism related to conservation areas and direct compensation for loss of income from land turned over to conservation).
   (c) Intensive farming practices may have a lasting detrimental impact on surrounding conservation estate. The financial rewards of conserving land may not compensate for the income lost through having unproductive land.

2. (a) Habitat loss (hedgerows and woodland areas).
   (b) Decline in abundance and diversity of food sources associated with habitat loss.

3. (a) In any order:
   − Hedgerow legislation to preserve existing hedgerows.
   − Policies to preserve or restore woodland cover in previously wooded areas (afforestation).
   − Schemes (with financial incentives) to encourage environmentally sensitive farming practices.
   (b) Environmental impact assessments and biodiversity estimates would determine the biodiversity levels and the environmental damage in certain habitats (e.g. areas with hedgerows vs areas where they had been removed or had become unkempt). This would identify areas requiring implementation of the biodiversity policies mentioned above, and also provide a baseline to measure the effectiveness of the strategies once implemented.

4. Retaining areas of uncultivated meadow alongside intensively managed pasture is helpful in that it boosts biodiversity in the area and can benefit agriculture in providing habitat for helpful insects, such as predators of pests and pollinators such as bumblebees. High diversity systems have better soil structure and cycle nutrients more efficiently, reducing fertiliser costs.

202. Hedgerows (page 273)

1. (a)-(c) any advantages of:
   − Hedgerows provide habitat and food for wildlife.
   − Hedgerows act as corridors along which animals can move between regions of suitable habitat (e.g. for feeding). Corridors are also important for the establishment and expansion of some plant species.
   − Hedgerows shelter stock and reduce wind speed, thereby reducing erosion.
   − Hedgerows provide habitat for pollinating insects and the predators of pest species. This may benefit the farmer.

2. Hedgerows might be regarded as undesirable because:
   − Hedgerows hamper effective use of some farm machinery.
   − Hedgerows take up space that could otherwise be used for grazing or crop production.
   − Hedgerows provide habitat for competitors to grazing livestock (e.g. hares) and predators (foxes).

3. Retaining well managed hedgerows offers the farmer many benefits. Hedges provide shelter for stock and reduce wind speeds, which stops erosion. Hedges provide habitat for helpful bird and insect species, which can prey on harmful pest insects and prevent spikes in pest populations. The also prevent the spread of wind-borne insect pests. Well managed hedges are also and eco-friendly cost-effective alternative to other types of fencing.

203. Quantifying Variation Using Student's t Test (page 274)

1. (a) The calculated t value is less than the critical value of t = 2.57. The null hypothesis cannot be rejected. There is no difference between control and experimental treatments.
   (b) The new t value supports the alternative hypothesis at P = 0.05 (reject the null hypothesis and conclude that there is a difference between the control and experimental treatments). Note the critical value of t in this case is 2.23 at 10 d.f. P = 0.05

2. Statistical significance refers to the probability that an observed difference (or trend) will occur by chance. It is an arbitrary criterion used as the basis for accepting or rejecting the null hypothesis in an investigation. **Note**: In science the term 'significantly different' has a specific meaning. It should not be used in a casual manner when no statistical test has been performed.

3. Step 1: H_0 there is no difference in heart rate between males and females. Step 2: Test two tailed.

   (a) Completed table:

x (bpm)		x − x̄ (deviation from mean)		(x − x̄)² (deviation from mean)²	
Male	Female	Male	Female	Male	Female
70	69	-2.3	1	5.29	1
74	62	1.7	-6	2.89	36
80	75	7.7	7	59.29	49
73	66	0.7	-2	0.49	4
75	68	2.7	0	7.29	0
82	57	9.7	-11	94.09	121
62	61	-10.3	-7	106.09	49
69	84	-3.3	16	10.89	256
70	61	-2.3	-7	5.29	49
68	77	-4.3	9	18.49	81
$n_A = 10$	$n_B = 10$			$\Sigma(x - \bar{x})^2$ 310.1	$\Sigma(x - \bar{x})^2$ 646

   (b) Variance of males: 34.45
       Variance of females: 71.78
   (c) Difference between groups means: 4.3
   (d) $t = 1.32$
   (e) Degrees of freedom: 18
   (f) $P = 0.05$, t (critical value) = 2.101
   (g) **Decision**: We cannot reject the null hypothesis; the difference between the two groups means is not significantly different at $P = 0.05$.

204. Quantitative Investigation of Variation (page 276)

x length / mm		x − x̄ (deviation from the mean)		(x − x̄)² (deviation from mean)²	
Paddock A	Paddock B	Paddock A	Paddock B	Paddock A	Paddock B
83	30	40.2	-77.5	1616.04	6006.25
70	87	27.2	-20.5	739.84	420.25
32	48	-10.8	-59.9	116.8	3543.1
61	92	18.2	-15.5	330.9	241.0
70	54	27.2	-53.5	739.3	2864.8
45	33	2.2	-74.5	4.8	5553.8
28	135	-14.8	27.5	219.3	754.9
34	60	-8.8	-47.5	77.6	2258.5
37	81	-5.8	-26.5	33.8	703.5
20	139	-33.8	31.5	520.3	990.8
25	90	-17.8	-17.5	317.2	307.1
30	78	-12.8	29.5	164.1	871.7
31	125	-11.8	17.5	139.5	305.4
35	174	-7.8	66.5	61.0	4419.1
80	167	37.2	59.5	1383.1	3537.4
22	184	-20.8	76.5	433.0	5848.6
62	80	19.2	-27.5	368.3	757.6
35	125	-7.8	17.5	61.0	305.4
25	163	-17.8	55.5	317.2	3077.6
44	197	1.2	89.5	1.4	8006.0
30	116	12.8	8.5	164.1	71.8
$n_A = 21$	$n_B = 21$			$\Sigma(x-\bar{x})^2$ 7807.2	$\Sigma(x-\bar{x})^2$ 50 849.2

Step 1
Population A: $\bar{x}_A = 42.8$ n = 21 $s_A = 19.76$
Population B: $\bar{x}_B = 107.5$ n = 21 $s_B = 50.4$

Step 2
Null hypothesis: There is no difference between the length of the clover stem in paddock A and paddock B

Step 3
Test is two tailed.

1. Variance population A = 390.45
   Variance population B = 2540.16
2. Difference between population means: -64.7
3. $t = -64.7 / \sqrt{((390.45/21) + 2540.16/21))} = -5.48$
4. d.f = 21 + 21 -2 = 40
5. P = 0.01 t = 2.704
6. 5.48 exceeds 2.704 so we can reject the null hypothesis.
7. There is a significant difference between the length of the clover stems in paddock A and B
8. Clover in paddocks A and B would need to be cut, dried, and weighed under the same 'cropping' regime. Therefore instead of using cattle, a mower with a catcher would need to used.

205. Investigating Genetic Diversity (page 278)

1. A DNA marker is a sequence of DNA that can be used to identify genes or differences in individuals.

2. Morphology is influenced by the environment as well as genetics making it difficult to tell if a feature is based on genetics or the environment. Similarly populations that look morphologically similar may be genetically diverse as some genetic characteristics may not cause obvious morphological differences between them.

3. (a) A fast evolving marker, e.g. variable tandem repeats.
   (b) A slow evolving marker, e.g. genes in the nuclear DNA.

206. Homologous DNA Sequences (page 279)

1. The similarity of DNA from different species can be established by measuring how closely single strands from each species mesh together. The more similar the DNA, the harder it is to separate them.

2. (a) Chimpanzee   (b) Galago

3. (a) 7 – 8   (b) Approx. 12

4. 45 million years ago.

207. Homologous Proteins (page 280)

1. Humans and rhesus monkeys are both primates and are more closely related to each other than either is to a horse, which is a mammal but not a primate.

2. (a) Highly conserved proteins are proteins that show very little change over time.
   (b) Proteins that are highly conserved tend to have critical roles within an organism (e.g. proteins involved in cellular respiration).
   (c) Any changes (mutations) to these proteins are likely to be harmful and stop the protein carrying out its function (and so are lethal).
   (d) Conserved proteins are probably homologous and therefore derived from a common ancestor. The few changes that are retained through time are likely to be meaningful, i.e. represent major divergences in evolutionary lines.

3. (a) The Pax-6 gene produces the Pax-6 protein which acts as a transcription factor to control the formation of some organs (including the eye) during embryonic development.
   (b) The Pax-6 gene from one species can be inserted into another and express a normally functioning protein. This is evidence that it is highly conserved.

208. Genetic Diversity in Springtails (page 282)

1. The TV11-14 group forms a distinct clade, which branched before the genetically distinct TV1-10 group (which is part of another clade that includes the Cape Royds, Cape Evans, and Beaufort Island groups). The TV1-10 group forms a cluster that is genetically closer than the other groups in the clade with which it shares a common ancestor.

2. The fact that the two types do not interbreed is significant because it means that reproductive isolating mechanisms have developed, or are in the process of developing. The two types may already be distinct species, or they could be in the process of diverging (if physical separation of the groups is the primary factor preventing their interbreeding).

3. Gene flow between populations will be very limited, if it occurs at all, because the springtails have very limited motility and are likely to die if blown any distance.

4. These conditions would have been ideal for the development of two species from a common ancestor. Small populations, isolated on mountain tops on either side of the valley, are likely to have had slight genetic differences and may then have been subjected to subtly different selection pressures (different microclimates etc.). The low dispersal (lack of gene flow) combined with the small population size, would have increased the differences between the isolated populations, which could then diverge genetically in a relatively short time.

209. Genetic Diversity in Endangered Populations (page 284)

1. Genetic diversity refers to the variety of alleles and genotypes present within a population.

2. (a) ADA enzyme locus
   (b) 6 / 26 = 0.23

3. (a) Low population numbers meant that there was a high degree of inbreeding. As a result, fertility rates (and production of viable offspring) decreased. This further decreased population numbers, making the inbreeding problem worse.
   (b) The introduced birds increased genetic diversity and increased genetic fitness of the population (more viable offspring were produced, so population numbers increased).

210. Chapter Review (page 285)

No model answer. Summary is the student's own.

211. KEY TERMS: Did You Get it? (page 287)

1. adaptation (H), biodiversity (L), binomial nomenclature (G), exon (B), crossing over (F), homologous chromosome (A), meiosis (C), mutation (E), natural selection (J), phylogeny (I), pre-RNA (K), recombination (D)

2. (a) A phenotype at the extreme of the phenotypic range has the greatest fitness so the phenotypic norm shifts in the direction of that phenotype. Example: selection in dark morphs in *Biston* moths in England during the Industrial Revolution.
   (b) Fitness is highest for the most common phenotype and there is selection against phenotypes at the extremes of the phenotypic range. Example: human birth weights.

2. (a) Mean population A = 1.26
       Mean population B = 1.11
   (b) s_A = 0.14 s_B = 0.20
   (c) t = 2.10
   (d) Degrees of freedom = 20. critical t value at 0.05 = 2.086. At this level of probability there is a significant difference in the populations (but not at 0.01 level of probability).

4. Kingdom, phylum, class, order, family, genus, species.